CHURCHILL:
Portrait of Greatness

by
Relman Morin

PRENTICE-HALL, Inc., Englewood Cliffs, N.J.

Winston Churchill's story reads like fiction, and not always believable fiction, rather than the record of a man's life. He was a headstrong boy who resisted books and schooling yet developed into a masterful writer. As a semi-educated cavalryman in India, he felt the urge to read history and became an accomplished historian himself. The fugitive in South Africa, "wanted, dead or alive," by sheerest chance knocked at the right door and it led him to his desired career. The patrician bachelor in London, instead of marrying a fortune, married a girl without a fortune, and "lived happily ever after." Several times, he was considered "finished" in politics, but he rebounded to win the highest office in Britain and the highest honors in the world. His father, Lord Randolph Churchill, was a brilliant and successful politician. Churchill not only survived the impact of this powerful personality but also surpassed his father's success in politics. Finally, onrushing events welded the talents and experience of the soldier, writer, politician, administrator, and student of geopolitics into one—the statesman who dwarfed all the others of this century. Here is material for several novels; it is only part of the history of Winston Churchill.

Churchill has said that the three decades between the beginning of World War I in 1914, and the end of World War II in 1945, "comprise and express my life-effort." In these seismic years, the world saw two Great Wars and the Great Depression, the shattering of old political patterns, the end of the Colonial Era, the growth of Communist power in the East, the ascendancy of the United States in the West. Churchill's footprints are everywhere in the mighty sequence of events. However, he had made his mark before 1914, and his influence by no means disappeared in 1945.

FULFILLMENT

THE EXPECTED MESSAGE CAME IN mid-afternoon. It requested him to present himself at Buckingham Palace at six o'clock. Shortly before the appointed hour, since his office in the Admiralty was nearby, Winston Churchill left for the Palace. He was taken at once to King George VI.

The business at hand was serious, but the King chose to open the audience on a note of banter.

"I suppose you don't know why I have sent for you," he said.

Churchill, of course, did know. (How many times, even as a boy, had he pictured this moment?) However, he tuned his reply to the King's chord. "Sir," he said, "I couldn't possibly imagine why."

The King laughed. Then he said, "I want to ask you to form a Government."

Thus, on May 10, 1940, Winston Churchill came to the office of Prime Minister and realized the fulfillment of his life's dream. No other moment would ever be charged with greater meaning for him.

It was a supremely critical moment.

In the darkness of May 9-10, the German armies had launched a mighty offensive against Holland and Belgium, and moved into position to attack France through the Ardennes Forest, a supposedly unlikely route of assault. For months, they had been inactive, coiled behind the Siegfried Line. The Germans were regrouping, of course, after the conquest of Poland. Huge placards, facing the French troops, assured them in their own language, "We will riposte only to your attack." Suddenly, they struck.

With a speed never before seen in war, the German armored columns began rumbling westward. Not long after the breakthrough, General Erwin Rommel, the great Panzer commander, swept forward as much as 40 miles in a single day. Inexorably, the avalanche of steel thundered toward the heart of France, toward the English Channel, toward a flat, undistinguished stretch of beach that would soon be immortalized in British history—Dunquerque.

So the Battle of Europe began, in surprise, confusion and terror.

Politically, the British reacted with equal speed.

When the grim tidings reached London, it became apparent that a National Government alone, a coalition rather than a party regime, was necessary to confront this emergency. Prime Minister Neville Chamberlain called several conferences on the morning of May 10. Churchill attended. By noon, it was all over. Chamberlain resigned and advised the King to turn to Winston Churchill.

After receiving the mandate to form a Government, Churchill returned to Admiralty House. Telegrams and messages were pouring in from the Continent. On huge, plastic-covered maps in the War Rooms, curving arrows, broken lines and colored symbols marked the positions of the armies, swaying in combat. A portrait of disaster was beginning to take shape on the maps.

Churchill worked on until long after midnight. Finally, he rose from his desk.

London, for the moment, slept peacefully. The hum of traffic long since had died down to a whisper. The spacious avenues and noble squares of the city, blacked out, were dark pools of silence. It was nearly 3 A.M.

Years later, Churchill recorded his feelings in that awesome hour—

"I felt as if I were walking with Destiny, and that all my past life had been but a preparation for this hour and for this trial . . . I thought I knew a good deal about it all, and I was sure I should not fail."

In all of Churchill's passages, written or spoken, nothing is more self-revealing than this extraordinary statement.

He was sixty-five years old in 1940. At that age, most men are retired, willingly or otherwise. Few can claim to still retain the energy, resourcefulness, and the creative powers they had possessed twenty years earlier. Yet here was Churchill at sixty-five, confidently, happily assuming his country's highest office, and shouldering the crushing burden of a World War, to boot.

He appears to have been endowed, from his earliest years, with the priceless gift of complete self-assurance. This is the mark of an aristocrat, which he was. When plans, military or political, miscarried *he* was always right and his critics were invariably wrong. He seems never to have doubted either his abilities or his judgment. To his critics, however, this enormous self-assurance was something else.

In the First World War, a London newspaper said of him:

"He sees himself as the only digit in the sum of things; all other men are mere ciphers. Indulged by the larger opportunity of a world-wide war, his instinct for the melodramatic has blossomed into megalomania."

At about the same time, Lord Grey, the Foreign Secretary, said of Churchill, "Winston very soon will become incapable, from sheer activity of mind, of being anything in a Cabinet but Prime Minister."

Now that ambition, the ambition of his life, had been crowned.

And there was a good deal of truth in his feeling that "all my past life had been but a preparation" for the task at hand. He came to it superbly equipped. His many-sided experiences all served to prepare him to be Britain's

6

chief at the time of her greatest peril. No other head of Government in the world had so wide-ranging a background for leadership in the greatest of wars.

First, the military side.

Churchill's career began in the Army. He knew combat and the hardships of the field. He had studied war. He first came to public attention in Britain by writing about war. He adapted tactics to new weapons. He thought in global terms, of naval and air bases, the sources of oil, and strategic positions. He learned to act decisively—rashly, his critics said—but at least with boldness and authority.

His military adventures opened the way for him to enter Parliament at the age of twenty-five. There he learned the rough-and-tumble of politics, the intricate and often cumbersome system that makes a democracy function.

This, in turn, led him to administrative office, where he dealt with foreign problems in the Colonial Office and domestic problems as head of the Board of Trade and Home Secretary. Long before 1940 Churchill was well schooled in the machinery of Government.

Most important, perhaps, he had developed to the "nth" degree his inherent ability to arouse emotion, to inspire and to encourage. Who else could have galvanized the British people when they stood alone, persuading them that their darkest hour was, in fact, their "finest hour"?

When you examine the long record—the little boy playing with tin soldiers, the young officer brushing death in combat, the politician-statesman of sixty-five becoming Prime Minister in wartime—a consistent pattern seems to emerge. Destiny? Is there some mysterious force that shapes the lives of men to be the instruments of its special purpose? Churchill himself, like other great captains, believed in his star. "I felt as if I were walking with Destiny." And of an earlier episode, he wrote, "Over me beat the invisible wings."

At any rate, he went to bed in the early hours of May 11, at the outset of the mightiest phase of his career, and recalled later, "Although impatient for the morning, I slept soundly."

A BACKWARD BOY

On THE NIGHT OF NOVEMBER 30, 1874, there was a great ball at Blenheim Palace, the castle given by Queen Anne to her redoubtable military commander, John Churchill, the first Duke of Marlborough. Among the guests was Lady Randolph Churchill, a bride of seven and one-half months. She attended against the advice of her physician.

Lady Randolph was American, a famous beauty, sparkling, gay, an immediate success in London society.

In the year before, Lord Randolph Henry Spencer-Churchill had written his father, the seventh Duke of Marlborough, about a girl from New York named Jennie Jerome. He confessed that he had known her only forty-eight hours. "Mr. Jerome," the letter continued, "is a gentleman who is obliged to live in New York to look after his business. I do not know what it is."

Nor, of course, did Lord Randolph know much about the beautiful American. But he was anxious to marry her—and at once.

Leonard Jerome was a millionaire and a man of many parts.

Among his other activities, he was a part-owner of *The New York Times*. He mounted cannon in the building during the riots of 1862 in New York. They seem not to have been used. Jerome also built a private opera house for himself, and he is said to have named his daughter after Jenny Lind, "the Swedish nightingale." His wife and daughters were living in a villa at Cowes, on the Isle of Wight, when Lord Randolph met Jennie Jerome, as she now spelled her name.

After some parental backing-and-filling on both sides, and after the Duke had gone to Paris to see the girl who had bewitched his son, the

The England in which Churchill grew up was exuberant, self-confident, and banker to the world. Seen here is Queen Victoria's Diamond Jubilee celebration, outside the steps of St. Paul's, in 1897. The future Prime Minister was then 23; Victoria had four more years to reign.

John Churchill, first Duke of Marlborough (1650-1720), victor over Louis XIV, founded the family from which Winston Churchill stemmed.

couple were married. Their wedding took place in the British Embassy in Paris, April 15, 1874.

On the night of the ball at Blenheim Palace, Lady Randolph suddenly disappeared. She hurried through long, cavernous corridors toward her bedroom. The story is that she was forced to stop before she could reach it. In a chamber being used that night as a ladies' cloak room, she gave birth to her first son, Winston Churchill.

Several days later, the London *Times* reported on page one: "On the 30th Nov. at Blenheim Palace, the Lady Randolph Churchill, was delivered prematurely, of a son."

1874 . . .

Victoria, Queen of the United Kingdom of Great Britain and Ireland, Empress of India, was in the thirty-seventh year of her reign. Her Prime Minster, Disraeli, had acquired shares in the Suez Canal, and the British flag fluttered over many parts of Asia and Africa. British policy was directed primarily at thwarting the designs of Czarist Russia. An English music hall song—

"We don't want to fight, but by Jingo, if we do,

"We got the ships, we got the men, we got the money, too."

It was quite true. Britain was at the zenith of power in the world. Figuratively, the Government was prepared to send a warship if someone knocked an Englishman's hat off anywhere in the world. Cavalrymen still wielded sabers in combat. The machines of war, the instruments of mass slaughter, were not yet developed. Battles were fought more by professionals than citizen-soldiers. "Pax Britannica."

England was pretty much ruled by a few hundred families, interlocked by marriage, and there was a great chasm between this "Establishment" and those who were not part of it. It was a world of caste, privilege, and wealth. (The Churchills, however, were not rich.)

This was the Britain into which Churchill was born. He started life with great advantages but his achievements came from his own efforts.

Winston Leonard Spencer Churchill, although inexorably British, the very personification of John Bull, physically and mentally, nevertheless cherished his American blood. In 1941, he addressed a joint session of Congress, reminded his audience that he was half-American, and added with a straight face:

"I like to reflect that if my father had been an American and my mother British, instead of the other way around, I might have got here [to Congress] on my own."

In 1900, when Churchill was on a lecture tour in the United States, Mark Twain introduced him with the words, "I give you the son of an American mother and an English father—the perfect man."

As a boy, however, there were no indications that he was equipped to go anywhere in politics, much less that he was "perfect." On the contrary, he was considered backward.

"He rather resembles a naughty little sandy-haired bulldog and seems backward except for complicated games with toy soldiers," said Grandmother Jerome.

Because of his reddish hair, his schoolmates called him "Carrots." A slightly protruding lower lip gave him a pouty look which he never outgrew. Nor did he ever outgrow the slight lisp: He called a cigar a "shigar."

From the first, he was fearless and physically tough as a wild boar. Considering the mishaps that befell him, it is a miracle that he lived to see his thirtieth birthday, let alone his sixty-fifth.

When he was five, he fell off a donkey and suffered a brain concussion. A few years later, finding himself trapped on a bridge in a game in which "Indians" were pursuing him, he jumped for the branches of a nearby tree. He miscalculated and crashed twenty-nine feet to the bottom of a rocky ravine. (In *My Early Life,* he confessed: "The argument was correct. The data were absolutely wrong.") He lay unconscious for three days and was in bed three months with a ruptured kidney.

As a soldier, of course, he was shot at, shelled and attacked with spears and swords. A taxi knocked him unconscious on Fifth Avenue in New York. And, as will be shown, he wandered through the wilderness of South Africa with a price (£25) on his head, "dead or alive."

He could well say, "over me beat the invisible wings."

In *Nuda Veritas,* Churchill's cousin, Clare Sheridan, says he was considered headstrong as a small boy. She recalled that "Winston had threatened, if he could not get his own way, that he would—and he searched his mind for the one thing that would strike his nurse as wickedest—'go and worship idols.' But he had a heart, for once when he had shot a small bird with an airgun, he was overcome with remorse and wept at bedtime."

The story of Churchill's first exposure to schooling is a curious one. The man who developed into one of the great masters of the English language, and became a passionate student of history, seems to have resisted education in the beginning. As he put it later, "I was *menaced* with education."

On the day when a Governess was to arrive to begin tutoring him, he "hid in the shrubs." He said that a book, *Reading Without Tears,* was the basis for his first lessons, but, "It certainly did not justify its title in my case."

Eventually, in the English custom, he was sent away to school. In *My Early Life,* he wrote:

"How I hated this school, and what a life of anxiety I lived there for more than two years. My teachers saw me at once backward and pre-

Jennie Jerome, Sir Winston's mother, was a great beauty and the daughter of an American, Leonard Jerome, principal owner of the *New York Times.* "She shone for me like the Evening Star," Churchill wrote in later years.

cocious, reading books beyond my years and yet at the bottom of the form."

Later, many institutions awarded him honorary degrees and Churchill frequently pointed to the irony of this. On one such occasion, he said:

"I am surprised that in later life I should have become so experienced in taking degrees when, as a schoolboy, I was so bad at passing examinations."

Elsewhere, he said, "I remained [in the same class] three times as long as anyone else."

The explanation seems twofold. "Where my reason, imagination or interest were not engaged, I would not or I could not learn," he said. Secondly, he was a late starter. It was not until he was in his twenties, a cavalry officer in India, that he realized his deficiencies. Then he said, simply, "The desire of learning came upon me."

He stayed at Harrow, the school for the sons of upper-class families, for more than four years.

Born in Brooklyn in 1854, Jennie Jerome spent her earliest years in Trieste, where her father was American Consul. After their return to the United States, the Jerome family occupied this house at the corner of 26th Street and Madison Avenue in New York City. It later became the Jockey Club and is now the Manhattan Club.

There, like many another schoolboy, he indulged in a mild form of cheating. He "concluded an alliance" with a classmate, who provided him with translations of his Latin lessons in exchange for essays composed by Churchill. "I used to walk up and down the room dictating—just as I do now—and he sat in the corner and wrote it all down in long-hand," Churchill said. "The arrangement worked admirably."

He won a school prize for reciting 1200 lines of Macaulay's *Lays of Ancient Rome* from memory. But aside from this, he said, "Except in fencing, in which I won the public school championship, I achieved no distinction."

Thus, his father concluded that his son was unfit for a career in law or politics. What then? The obvious answer was the Army.

This decision came, Churchill said, when his father watched him playing with his tin soldiers. Winston, with his brother Jack (1880-1947), collected 1500 of these. Clare Sheridan wrote—

"The playroom contained from one end to the other a plank table on trestles, upon which were thousands of lead soldiers arranged for battle. He organized wars . . . it was a most impressive show and played with an interest that was no ordinary game."

Lord Randolph, after watching one of these Homeric conflicts for some twenty minutes, asked his son if he would like to go into the Army.

"Yes," the boy replied. And that decided it. "The toy soldiers turned the current of my life," Churchill said.

But he was no more successful in passing the examinations for Sandhurst, the British equivalent of the United States Military Academy, than he had been in his other schools. Twice he failed. Then, with the help of a tutor, a retired Army officer, he qualified on the third try. Since he was interested in his studies now, as contrasted to his lack of interest in conventional schooling, Churchill was a success at Sandhurst. He graduated in a class of 150 and was commissioned a lieutenant in a cavalry regiment, the Fourth Hussars.

It seems clear, however, that Winston Churchill even earlier had started dreaming of a career elsewhere than in the Army—politics. Churchill later said, "I am a child of the House of Commons."

How could a "backward boy," a poor student, resistant to learning, aspire to a place in "the Mother of Parliaments"? The answer probably lies in his environment and in qualities that were to lie dormant for several more years.

Lord Randolph Churchill was a powerful and stormy figure in the House of Commons. He had been leader of the House, Chancellor of the Exchequer, and an influential member of the Conservative Party. Political leaders often were guests in the Churchill home. The boy heard

Keystone

Blenheim Palace, in Oxfordshire, containing some 320 rooms, was presented to John Churchill, first Duke of Marlborough, by Queen Anne. During a ball at the Palace in 1874, Lady Randolph raced over a quarter mile to the ladies' cloakroom and gave birth prematurely to a son, who would be christened Winston Leonard Spencer Churchill.

Two-year-old Winston poses with his mother in his earliest known photograph, 1876, the year when the Churchills went to Ireland where Lord Randolph became secretary to his father, the Lord-Lieutenant.

British Information Services

Lord Randolph Churchill, Winston's father, was the third son of the seventh Duke of Marlborough. By the age of 36 he had become leader of the House of Commons and Chancellor of the Exchequer. He died when Winston was 21.

Radio Times Hulton Picture Library

By the age of six, Winston had acquired the nickname "Carrots," for his sandy hair. In that year (1880), "we were all thrown out of office by Mr. Gladstone," he was later to write.

By 1889 he had been a schoolboy at Harrow for three years. An indifferent student, he said "the subjects which were dearest to the examiners were almost invariably those I fancied least."

Lady Randolph Churchill, in 1889, with Winston and his younger brother Jack.

As a subaltern at the Royal Military Academy, Sandhurst, he wears full dress uniform of the Fourth Queen's Own Hussars.

With his mother, and wearing a large straw hat, Winston is seen at a garden party
given by Sir Whittaker and Lady Ellis at Buccleuch House, Richmond, about 1886.

discussions of politics in his earliest years. Later, he went to the House and listened, enthralled, to the debates.

An incident, when Churchill was thirteen, is illuminating. The Prince of Wales asked him playfully, "How would you like to be Prince of Wales?"

The boy replied, "I would rather be Prime Minister."

In this connection, it should be noted that at the time, Churchill was next in line of succession to be Duke of Marlborough. The American heiress, Consuelo Vanderbilt, who became the Duchess, said in her memoirs that when she arrived in England as a bride the Duke's grandmother sternly informed her:

"Your first duty is to have a child and it must be a son, because it would be intolerable to have that little upstart, Winston, become Duke. Are you in the family way?"

The old dowager's anxieties were groundless. If, as it appears, Churchill's ambitions centered on the House of Commons even as a teen-ager, he would have attempted to avoid becoming Duke. The title would have disqualified him for the House. Years later, he refused a title for that very reason.

He imagined himself in the House, allied with his father, fighting the great battles that swirled around Lord Randolph. This was not to be. In 1895, when Winston was twenty, his father died.

"All my dreams were ended," Churchill wrote. "There remained for me only to pursue his aims and vindicate his memory."

As a young M.P., Churchill did in fact take his father's position in a great debate on military

economy, and, at the risk of reopening old wounds, referred to his father by name.

Yet, as a boy, father and son do not appear to have been close.

Churchill said he found himself shy and tongue-tied in the presence of his father. He recalled how greatly he envied one of his classmates who conversed easily with Lord Randolph. Of himself on those occasions, he said, "I was only a backward boy and my incursions into the conversation were nearly always awkward or foolish."

Once, he said, his father "warned me of the danger in which I plainly lay of becoming a social wastrel. I was pained." Elsewhere, he said he had "three or four intimate conversations with him, which are all I can boast."

Of his mother, he said:

"She made a brilliant impression upon my childhood life. She shone for me like the evening star. I loved her dearly, but at a distance. She always seemed to me a fairy princess."

When he was in the Army and pulling strings to further his career, he did not hesitate to ask his mother to use her connections in London on his behalf. This she did in full measure. He said:

"Indeed she soon became an ardent ally, furthering my plans and guarding my interest with all her influence and boundless energy. We worked together on even terms, more like brother and sister than mother and son."

At twenty-one, he went to Cuba where he came under rifle fire for the first time, and then to India where he took the first faltering steps toward greatness.

"I WAS EAGER FOR TROUBLE"

THE FIRST TIME CHURCHILL EVER heard shots fired in anger was very nearly the last time. He was in Cuba and the incident took place on his twenty-first birthday. It made him "thoughtful," he said, but it did not deter him from continuing to pursue wars and adventure in the ensuing years. In fact, he never lost his taste for danger. Nearly a half-century later, he planned secretly to sail with the assault forces in the invasion of Normandy. The plot, to his bitter disappointment, fell through.

He went to Cuba as an observer with the Spanish Army to watch a rebellion. There, he discovered what few European or American military men understood at the time, the potency of guerrilla warfare. The experience was to prove invaluable during the Boer War.

By 1895, Churchill had been commissioned a lieutenant in the Queen's Fourth Hussars. The unit was given six months' leave before sailing for India. Churchill persuaded a brother-officer, Lieutenant Reginald Barnes, to go with him to Cuba. He wanted to see real warfare and, more important, to write about it. We come to the writing shortly.

On November 30, 1895, near the village of Arroyo Blanco, a volley of rifle shots from the jungle raked the Spanish camp. A bullet whizzed close to Churchill's head—within less than a foot, he said—and killed a horse near which he was standing. He wrote, ". . . I had been under fire. That was something. Nevertheless, I began to take a more thoughtful view of our enterprise."

Now the writing.

Churchill always needed money, or said he did, as a boy in school and as a subaltern. In the Cuban adventure, he saw the opportunity to have some fun and at the same time earn some money. So before he sailed, he made an arrangement with the London *Daily Graphic* to serve as a war correspondent in the Rebellion. Whether he could write, of course, was yet to be seen. He had written for the school magazine at Harrow, but not for any commercial publications. In any case, he "sold" the editors of the *Daily Graphic* on himself. He was to receive £5 per article. No doubt Lady Randolph's connections in London played a part here, as they were to do more than once.

The *Daily Graphic* published five articles on the Rebellion by Churchill, some running well over a column.

These reports constitute his first "professional" writing. They were the seeds of the career that made Churchill, in the words of one of his editors, "the finest writer I ever knew." Very soon, in India, Egypt, and in South Africa, he would be writing about what he called "Britain's little wars." Churchill the writer was the child of a love affair between Ares and Clio.

A war correspondent's fame is fleeting, at best, but Churchill expanded his newspaper reports into books. They quickly brought him to the attention of the British public, to military men (who frequently were infuriated by his criticisms) and to the major British political leaders of the day. They led him directly to his first goal, a seat in the House of Commons.

Before that, however, a remarkable flowering of personality took place.

The Fourth Hussars sailed for India in 1896. Disembarking in Bombay, Churchill slipped on the stone steps of the quay and dislocated his shoulder. In other eras, this would have been interpreted as an unfavorable omen. Churchill thought so, too. The injury handicapped him in polo. He played with his arm strapped to his side, but nevertheless was instrumental in winning a regimental championship in India.

And instead of wielding a saber in combat, he had to use a pistol, a fact that probably saved his life in the Battle of Omdurman.

The Hussars were garrisoned at Bangalore, in the hills. The climate was good. Life was unhurried. For Churchill and his brother-officers, it consisted primarily of duty and polo.

It was during these days, as Churchill put it so simply, that "The desire of learning came upon me."

He has only partially explained this mysterious development. He was twenty-two years old. As a schoolboy, he had resisted the very thing

Graduating from Sandhurst eighth in a class of 150, young Winston, now commissioned a second lieutenant, looked about for a war to fight. First going to Cuba as an observer with the Spanish Army, he later joined the Fourth Hussars in India (above), where he saw active service.

he now desired. Why? A restlessness of intellect? A late flowering? All Churchill himself said in his book, *My Early Life,* was that he became interested in words and the structure of the English sentence. He said he caught himself using words whose meanings he did not truly know. He cited "ethics" as an example, and wrote:

"Of tactics, I had a grip. On politics, I had a view. But ethics? . . . I resolved to read history, philosophy and economics."

He wrote his mother and asked for books from London. Soon, he was reading Plato, Socrates and Schopenhauer, Malthus, Darwin and Lecky. But it was the historians, Macaulay and Gibbon, who influenced him most.

Writers seldom acknowledge consciously imitating other writers, but Churchill candidly wrote:

"I affected a combination of the styles of Macaulay and Gibbon . . . and I stuck in a bit of my own from time to time."

In 1897, while he was in England on leave, he learned that trouble had broken out with Pathan tribesmen on the Northwest Frontier in India and that an expeditionary force was being organized. He knew the commanding officer, Sir Bindon Blood, and promptly telegraphed his desire to join the expedition. The general replied that he could come to the Frontier as a war correspondent.

Churchill obtained a commission to report the operation for the Allahabad newspaper, *Pioneer,* and his mother arranged for him to report for the *Daily Telegraph* in London, as well.

In the action on the Frontier, Churchill was more than a war correspondent. He commanded troops of a unit which, having been badly chewed up by the Pathans, was left with only three English officers. Churchill was involved in some vicious fighting.

Out of his dispatches on this action came his first book, *The Story of the Malakand Field Force. An Episode of Frontier War.*

The book was a great success, widely reviewed and highly praised. Churchill, of course, was delighted and somewhat overcome. In *My Early Life,* he wrote:

"I had never been praised before. The only comments which had been made upon my work at school had been 'indifferent,' 'untidy,' 'slov-

When the Boer War broke out in 1899, Churchill went to South Africa as a special war correspondent for the *Morning Post,* after an unsuccessful bid for Parliament.

enly,' 'bad,' 'very bad,' and so on. Now here was the great world with its leading literary newspapers and vigilant erudite critics writing whole columns of praise."

He even received a "fan letter" from the Prince of Wales. "My dear Winston," the Prince wrote, "I have read it with the greatest possible interest and I think the descriptions and language generally excellent. Everybody is reading it . . ."

Churchill promptly came to a decision. As soon as possible (winning the Polo Cup in India was one consideration) he would leave the Army, support himself by writing, and stand for the House of Commons.

From that moment, writing became a way of life with him. There was always a book waiting to be written, regardless of his other activities. He was immensely prolific and could no more avoid writing, contemporary history or events in the past, than he could stop breathing.

Next, he tried creative writing. He turned out a novel, *Savrola*, which had a mild success. At least it went into several reprintings, the last time being on his eightieth birthday in 1954. It was his only novel, and quite probably it reveals something of the mind and soul of an ambitious young man. He has his hero offering some solutions to life's problems:

"Would you rise in the world? You must work while others amuse themselves. Are you desirous of a reputation for courage? You must risk your life. Would you be strong, physically or morally? You must resist temptation.

"All this is paying in advance."

Reviewers of the book were quick to note that *Savrola* had no love-story worthy of the name. The reason, no doubt, was that Churchill had formed no romantic attachments. Another decade would pass before he did, and then it lasted all his life.

In any case, he made these advance payments on success in good measure.

Churchill was known to be a formidable drinker and in this connection it is interesting to speculate on an assertion he made later about his habits in his youth.

Dean Acheson, former Secretary of State, reported the incident in an article in *The Saturday Evening Post*.

Acheson said that in 1952, when Churchill was seventy-eight, President Truman gave a dinner for him aboard, the yacht, *Williamsburg*. At dinner, Churchill claimed that, from the age of sixteen to that evening, he had consumed on the average about a quart of wines and spirits a day.

He wondered, Acheson said, how high in the room the tide would rise if the total volume of all those emptied bottles were poured into it. Lord Cherwell, an eminent British scientist who was present, made some quick calculations. "Just under two and a half feet," he said. Acheson wrote:

The young correspondent was captured by the Boers when an armored train on which he and two companies of infantry were riding was derailed.

Churchill, at extreme right, was photographed after being taken by the Boers and marched sixty miles to a prisoner-of-war camp in Pretoria. "We don't catch the son of a lord every day," crowed his captors.

"The results were very disappointing to the old man. He had expected that we would all be swimming like goldfish in a bowl, whereas it would hardly come up to our knees."

Well, Churchill had an iron constitution. But can you picture him, even as a robust young officer, writing for three or four hours daily in India while working his way through an average of a quart of wine and spirits? Anyway, it was a good story.

Photographs taken in that period of his life show Churchill as a lean, square-shouldered youth, handsome in a brocaded regimental uniform. His gaze is long and steady, and the square chin is frankly aggressive. He had a pencil-thin moustache. His lower lip is slightly protruding, faintly petulant. It saves him from an expression of icy hauteur.

And here is how the Boers saw him when they issued a "wanted-dead-or-alive" poster after Churchill escaped from a prisoner-of-war camp:

"Englishman, twenty-five years old, about five feet eight inches tall, indifferent build, walks with a forward stoop, pale appearance, red-brownish hair, small and hardly noticeable moustache, talks through his nose, cannot pronounce the letter 's,' properly." (A reference to his lisp.)

At about this period of his life, there was another interesting development. "I passed through a violent and aggressive anti-religious phase," he said, apparently as a result of reading what is sometimes called "higher criticism." He continued:

"However, my poise was restored during the next years by frequent contact with danger. I did not hesitate to ask for special protection when about to come under the fire of the enemy, nor to be sincerely grateful when I came home."

How many soldiers could say the same!

Having passed through the "aggressive anti-religious phase," Churchill arrived at a quite different point of view.

"I have always been surprised," he wrote, "to see some of our bishops and clergy making such heavy weather about reconciling the Bible story with modern scientific and historical knowledge. Why do they want to reconcile them?

"If you are the recipient of a message which cheers your heart and fortifies your soul, which promises reunion with those you have loved in a world of larger opportunity and wider sympathies, why should you worry about the shape or color of the travel-stained envelope?"

In a kind of summing-up, he added, "The idea that nothing is true except what we comprehend is silly."

The next "contact with danger" came in 1898. Churchill got wind of another impending military operation, an expedition to Khartoum in the Sudan against the Dervish Empire. It was to be led by Sir Herbert Kitchener. Churchill's reflexes moved instantly. He must accompany that force. He must write about the campaign.

He applied for a transfer from India to Egypt. The request was refused. Thereupon, he returned to London on leave.

It was the mixture as before. Lady Randolph set about to pull strings in official circles. She knew Kitchener and she wrote him on behalf of her son. A polite refusal came back. Everywhere they turned, mother and son met blank walls. Churchill was convinced that his dispatches and *The Story of the Malakand Field Force* had aroused resentment in Army circles. To him, it seemed clear that Kitchener did not want Lieutenant Churchill to observe *his* campaign and probably to second-guess *his* tactics. At least, the young man was now well known.

But if the book hindered Churchill in one quarter, it gave him the necessary leverage in another to get what he wanted. The Prime Minister, Lord Salisbury, read it and said he would like to meet the author.

As the interview ended, Salisbury said, "I hope you will allow me to say how much you remind me of your late father, with whom such important days of my political life were lived. If there is anything at any time that I can do which would be of assistance to you, pray do not fail to let me know."

Not long afterward, Churchill found himself assigned to the Twenty-first Lancers and hotfooting it for Cairo. He had time first, however, to sign on with the London *Morning Post* for a series of articles. Now the price had gone up. He was to receive £15 per report.

At sunrise, on September 2, 1898, the Battle of Omdurman began. In about five hours, the Dervish forces were routed. Churchill's unit, the Lancers, rode out in pursuit. They were cut off and surrounded by several thousand of the enemy. Churchill vividly described how the cavalrymen were dragged from their horses and "cut to pieces." Because of his old injury, he was unable to use his sword so he went into the action carrying a pistol. He was able to shoot his way through the melée. A Dervish attacked him with a spear. "I shot him at less than a yard," Churchill wrote. "How easy to kill a man!"

The campaign, of course, produced another book. Churchill had written thirteen dispatches from the Nile for the *Morning Post*. Again he expanded them. *The River War* was a much more comprehensive book than *The Malakand Field Force*. It reflected the development of his abilities and attracted still more attention to him.

He evidently thought the moment was propitious to try for the next goal. In 1899, at the age of twenty-four, he ran for the House as a Conservative Party candidate. He lost.

But in his second attempt, he succeeded. It can be said that Churchill entered the House through a door in South Africa.

The Boer War, long impending, broke out in the autumn of 1899. Churchill sailed for Capetown immediately. Again, the *Morning Post* commissioned him to report it. But now he was on salary and all his expenses were to be paid. Clearly, a new star had risen over Fleet Street.

Apart from that, as he said, "I was eager for trouble."

He found it. On November 15, 1899, the Boers captured him. In the next sequence of events, he became practically a national hero at home. He devoted nearly sixty pages to the story in a subsequent book. Briefly, this is what happened:

Churchill, looking for a story, went out with an armored train. The Boers, fine marksmen, quickly brought it under artillery fire and hit it with shrapnel shells. Retreating, several cars were derailed and the British sustained some casualties.

The rules of war forbid a war correspondent to carry arms or actually engage in combat operations. (Needless to say, the rule has often been broken.) Churchill did both on that day. He was carrying his pistol and, in effect, he took charge after the derailment. He had the locomotive unhooked, placed the wounded in the cab, and directed the engineer to withdraw.

As the locomotive gained speed, the other British troops fell behind. Churchill, under a hail of bullets, went back down the track to find them.

Two Boers rode toward him in a leisurely manner, covering him with rifles. He was a prisoner. One of his captors was Louis Botha, who also became Prime Minister of his country.

Fortunately for Churchill, he had lost his pistol in all the excitement. Being in civilian

20

clothes, he could have been executed for carrying arms in combat. He surreptitiously threw away several bullets. When the Boers saw him do it, he said he had picked them up on the field.

He tried to avoid imprisonment, arguing that he was a civilian. The Boers, however, had seen him actively working to free the locomotive. Besides, they said, "It isn't every day that we catch the son of an English lord." Into the prison camp he went.

His colleagues, of course, reported that he was missing in action. Then they learned he had been captured. It all made sensational reading in London.

About a month later, Churchill escaped. It was then that the Boers issued the "dead-or-alive" placard. Churchill later learned that the price on his head was only about $100 and he faintly resented it.

For days he wandered through the veldt, all Boer territory. Once he jumped for a moving train, slipped, and nearly fell beneath the wheels. At last, starving and desperate, he took the long chance and knocked on the door of a house in the open country.

Incredible luck always attended him. The house was occupied by Englishmen operating a mine. They were the only Englishmen for miles around. "Over me beat the invisible wings."

They hid him in the mine and then, covering him under a pile of coal sacks on a train bound for Portuguese East Africa, sent him on his way to freedom.

The news of his escape caused a sensation in London precisely because it contrasted so sharply with the other news from the war. The Army had suffered a succession of setbacks, some of them serious. Churchill's adventure was just the feat of derring-do to capture the imagination of a disgruntled people.

He further sharpened his public image with a series of articles, filed from Laurenço Marques in Portuguese East Africa, criticizing the composition of the British forces and the tactics employed against the Boers.

"The individual Boer," he wrote, "mounted in suitable country, is worth three to five regular soldiers." The observation echoed what he had seen of guerrilla warfare in Cuba.

Translation.

£25

(Twenty-five Pounds stg.) REWARD is offered by the Sub-Commission of the fifth division, on behalf of the Special Constable of the said division, to anyone who brings the escaped prisioner of war

CHURCHILL,

dead or alive to this office.

For the Sub-Commission of the fifth division.
(Signed) LODK. de HAAS, Sec.

NOTE.—The Original Reward for the arrest of Winston Churchill on his escape from Pretoria, posted on the Government House at Pretoria, brought to England by the Hon. Henry Massham, and is now the property of W. R. Barton.

In short order, Churchill escaped. Reward poster included a description: "Englishman about twenty-five years old, about five feet eight inches tall, indifferent build, walks with a forward stoop, pale appearance, reddish-brown hair, small and hardly noticeable mustache, talks through his nose and cannot pronounce the letter 's' properly."

He admitted that he was a "venomous amateur strategist."

These critical reports kicked up a storm in London. He was called a "medal snatcher" and "self-advertiser." With heavy-handed sarcasm, a newspaper said, "We have received no confirmation of the statement that Lord Lansdowne has, pending the arrival of Lord Roberts, appointed Mr. Winston Churchill to command the troops in South Africa." Some elderly officers in the "Buck and Dodder Club" sent Churchill a cable, "Best friends here hope you will not continue making ass of yourself."

21

A hero after his escape, Churchill was carried to the steps of the Town Hall in Durban, South Africa, and induced to deliver a speech. He was inundated with telegrams of congratulation from all over the world.

The net effect of so much newspaper discussion, pro and con, was to make Lieutenant Churchill the best-known subaltern in the Army. There was even a music hall song about him as a war correspondent. Glittering vistas in journalism opened.

Churchill's eyes were elsewhere. He would make his second try for a seat in the House of Commons. He had acquired such prominence now that he had his choice of any one of eleven districts. With his instinctive sense of drama, he chose Oldham, the scene of his original defeat. He won by an eyelash, a margin of 230 votes out of about 30,000 cast.

The year was 1900. He was not yet twenty-six. High office lay ahead.

THE POLITICIAN AND THE LADY

THE TWO BACHELORS, USING A secret code, amused themselves with a game that few of their lady friends in Edwardian London would have appreciated. The key to it was that poetic tribute to the beauty of Helen of Troy, she of "the face that launched 1000 ships." As each female guest entered the room at a social affair, the two men would speculate on the number of ships *her* face might have launched in the Trojan War.

"Two hundred, perhaps two hundred and fifty," one would say.

"By no means," the other would retort, "a small gunboat, at most."

The bachelors were Winston Churchill and his secretary and close friend of many years, Edward Marsh. In *The Age of Churchill*, Peter de Mendelssohn noted that very few British beauties of the day received the maximum number of ships in the estimation of Churchill and Marsh.

But there were some, and among them was Clementine Ogilvy Hozier.

She was tall and she carried herself like a queen. She had a chiselled profile, ash blonde hair arranged in a high, Gibson Girl pompadour, luminous grey eyes, a generous mouth, and a chin fully as firm as Churchill's. At first sight, Churchill and Marsh accorded Clementine Hozier the full "1000 ships."

Her father, who had died in 1907, was Sir Henry Montagu Hozier, a colonel in the British Army. Her mother was a daughter of the Earl of Airlie. For some years, and for reasons of economy, Lady Blanche Hozier and Clementine lived in a pension in France. It was at Dieppe, scene of the disastrous Allied raid in the early part of World War II. Clementine Hozier spoke fluent French and German.

London society, of course, considered Churchill an eminently good catch. Since he had no personal fortune, and politics was an expensive

Churchill met Clementine Hozier, his future bride, at a ball given by her grandmother, the Countess of Arlie, in 1908. The wedding took place the following September at St. Margaret's Church, in the yard of Westminster Abbey. The Churchills honeymooned first at Blenheim, later in Italy.

profession even in those days, it was generally expected that he would marry some wealthy man's daughter. No doubt he could have done so. He was a blue-blood, a Member of Parliament, and by 1908, already a Cabinet Minister. To add to this luster, he had enhanced his reputation as a writer when, in 1905, he brought out *Lord Randolph Churchill*, the biography of his stormy father. It is one of his best books.

In short, by 1908, Churchill already was something of a celebrity in England. He had an instinct for attracting attention. His maiden speech in the House had set tongues a-wagging. Britain was still fighting the Boers—much to the discomfort of the Tories—and this new Tory M.P. urged a policy of magnanimity! M.P.'s on both sides of the House blinked with surprise when the young man said, "Last but by no means least, the British Army would most readily accord to a brave foe all the honors of war." Well!

Next, Churchill left the Tories and crossed to the Liberals in 1904. When he rose to speak for the first time, a band of Tories virtually howled him down. (It would not be the last time.) He was only thirty, a very junior member, but he counterattacked so furiously that the Speaker ruled him out of order. Next, he fought in the forefront of the great Constitutional struggle against the House of Lords. This made him a "traitor to his class." An M.P. may have echoed the opinion of others in the House when he said of Churchill, "He is a formidable opponent but I would rather have him as an opponent than on my side."

Renown came so swiftly to Churchill that the first biography about him appeared when he was barely thirty, *Winston Spencer Churchill*, by A. MacCallum Scott. Today there are perhaps fifty such books.

It can even be said that Churchill's success may be gauged by the number of enemies he so quickly acquired. In *Winston Churchill*, Rene Kraus wrote, "He was now, even more than Lloyd George, the best-hated man in English conservative circles."

In his bachelor years in London, Churchill shared an apartment in Mayfair with his brother, Jack. It was small, cluttered with books, littered with papers. All his life, he liked to write in bed. He would stay up late for an interesting dinner,

but otherwise he would retire early to read or work. What was an interesting dinner? "My idea of a good dinner," he said, "is first to have good food, then to discuss good food, and after this good food has been discussed, to discuss a good topic—with myself as chief conversationalist."

Unlike many Englishmen of his class, he spent little time in his clubs. He permitted himself no leisure. If he went to a club or any social affair, he usually had a purpose. Recall *Savrola's* formula for success—"Would you rise in the world? You must work while others amuse themselves."

He was all energy, driving, single-minded, impatient, hungry for power, a comet rushing toward some unforeseeable political zenith.

Lord Randolph Churchill had died at a comparatively early age and, as a young man, Churchill seems to have felt that he would not have a long life, either. Whatever he was to accomplish, he said, must be done before he was forty. Hence, he must hurry.

This was the man Clementine Hozier met at a Mayfair dinner in 1908.

She was twenty-three. He was nearly eleven years older. A few weeks after they met, Churchill invited Miss Hozier to his birthplace, Blenheim Palace. He escorted her across the grounds to a pagoda on the edge of a lake. There, he proposed. (They revisited the spot on their Golden Wedding anniversary.) The wedding took place, September 12, 1908, in St. Margaret's, the official church of the House of Commons.

Churchill was anything but a flustered bridegroom. David Lloyd George, later to be Prime Minister, recalled that "Even at his wedding, Winston began talking politics in the vestry."

Some 800 guests attended. Crowds gathered outside the church. The King and Queen sent gifts and the Churchills received twenty-five candlesticks, twenty-one inkstands, twenty bowls, fifteen vases, jewelry glittering with rubies and diamonds, jade, and rare books. Descriptions of the ceremony and all this magnificence filled columns in the newspapers.

Churchill took his bride to Blenheim Palace for the first few days of their honeymoon. Then they went to Paris and Lago Maggiore in Italy. When they returned to London, they set up housekeeping in Eccleston Square, Victoria.

As Home Secretary in 1910, Churchill arrives at the law courts with Clementine to testify in a libel suit. A miners' strike and rioting Suffragettes kept him hopping that year.

Three daughters and a son were born to them, Marigold (who died at the age of three), Diana, Sarah, and Randolph.

In 1930, more than two decades later, Churchill wrote, ". . . and then I married and lived happily ever after." On their wedding anniversaries, he invariably proposed his toast "to my darling Clementine." Usually, he called her "Clemmie." In his old age, he paid her the ultimate tribute, "It would have been impossible for any ordinary man to go through what I have had to get through in peace and war without her devoted aid."

Her unqualified loyalty created a small contretemps not long after their marriage. At Blenheim Palace one day, her host, the Duke of Marlborough, began criticizing Herbert Asquith, the Liberal Party leader.

"You are not to say such things about Winston's leader," the new Mrs. Churchill said.

The Duke grumbled on.

"If you continue," she said, "I shall leave."

The Duke continued. She rose to leave, and although he apologized, she refused to return.

1908.

Politically, too, Churchill came to a milestone in that year. His first office in Government, Under-Secretary of State for the Colonies, was limited in scope. For him, that is. It could not contain his vaulting ambition nor provide an outlet for all his explosive energy. He held it for two years. Now, in 1908, he moved up to be President of the Board of Trade. In some respects, the office resembles the U.S. Department of Commerce. Churchill, forever reaching out for wider authority, expanded its scope so that, in effect, he also functioned as a Secretary of Labor.

He knew little about the workingman. Indeed, in his first campaign for Parliament in Oldham, a workingman's district, he looked a little foolish. He emphasized the glories of Britain while his opponent stressed "the misery of the working classes" and "the glaring contrast between riches and poverty."

But Churchill could quickly grasp the essentials of a problem and by 1908 he made the workingman his own.

25

With Mrs. Churchill and General Bruce Hamilton, the Home Secretary watches maneuvers at Aldershot in 1910.

A rough parallel emerges here between Churchill and Franklin Delano Roosevelt.

Each was born to privilege, to a station in life far removed from the lot of the poor and the not-privileged. Class lines, of course, were more sharply drawn in England than in the United States. Privilege, in the England of 1908, was largely a question of lineage; in the United States, wealth could open the door to the American "aristocracy." In both nations, a deep abyss yawned between those who were secure against unemployment, illness and economic exploitation, and those who were not. Private charity might care for the widows and orphans, the incapacitated, the aged, but Government did not. As a young man, Churchill had heard a dinner conversation between some other bright young men on the question, "Are people entitled to *self*-government, or merely *good* Government."

26

(He was later told they were not serious.) Their wealthy counterparts in America probably would have said either form would do, provided it was a Government of laissez-faire.

For instituting reforms in 1908, Churchill became a "traitor to his class." So did Roosevelt in 1932 and for the same reason.

It must have made strange reading for some of Churchill's friends, the aristocrats in the great homes of England, when they opened *The Times* one morning and found a scion of the Marlboroughs calling for—

"A Government which will think a little more about the toiler at the bottom of the mine and a little less about the fluctuations of the share market in London . . . a Government which will think the condition of a slum in an English city is not less worthy of attention than the jungle of Somaliland."

This sounds like a far cry from the Churchill who railed against "Socialism" after the Labor Party deposed the Tories in 1945. The apparent contradiction, however, may not be as sharp as it seems. For in one of those symmetrical sentences that he dearly loved to mold, Churchill said:

"The inherent vice of Capitalism is the unequal sharing of blessings; the inherent virtue of Socialism is the equal sharing of miseries."

So perhaps, basically, Churchill was what is called in the United States today a middle-of-the-roader.

In any case, as President of the Board of Trade, he identified himself with legislation that seemed startling, Socialistic, possibly dangerous in the England of that day: a Port of London Act to protect dock workers against exploitation, laws providing an eight-hour day for miners and a minimum wage for unskilled workers in "sweated" industries, labor exchanges to help the jobless man find a job, coupled with unemployment insurance. Much of this later merged into the National Insurance Act which covered illness and disablement for working-men.

The ideas were not wholly new; some had been debated for twenty years but not enacted into law. Nor were they wholly Churchill's; Lloyd George said Churchill snatched an idea from him, framed a bill and introduced it as his own.

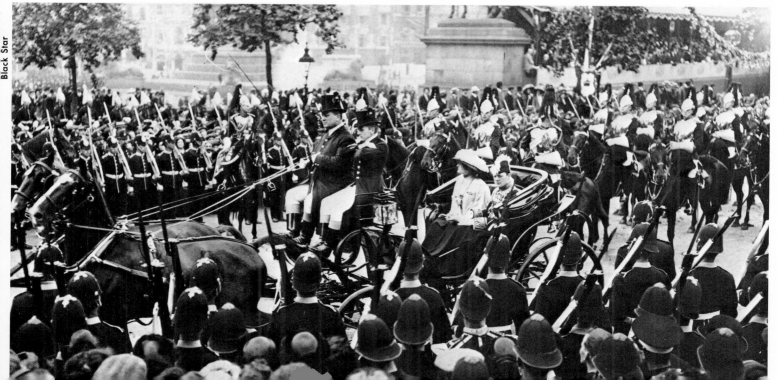

Churchill arrived on the scene in the "Battle of Sidney Street," in 1911. A group of anarchists, who had shot four police constables, were barricaded in a building. The Home Secretary set up battle headquarters, called in the troops. The anarchists died when their stronghold caught fire.

In this whole field, in some respects, Britain was unique in the world.

Thus the precursor of the cheer that rose so often during the Second World War, "Good old Winnie," first came from some unemployed workmen in a London suburb in 1910. Only they yelled, "Good old Churchill," although he was only thirty-five.

The next step was Home Secretary, a hydra-headed monster of an office. Nothing quite like it exists in the U.S. Government. The responsibilities attached to it were so numerous and so varied that in Washington they would be assigned to a half-dozen departments, bureaus and agencies—mines, fisheries, agriculture, prison administration, the London police and fire departments, control of liquor, firearms and dangerous drugs, responsibility for public safety and public morals.

The Home Secretary also was "His Majesty's Principal Secretary of State." This entailed composing a report for the King, summarizing each day's doings in Parliament. Churchill's résumés intrigued and amused Edward VII; occasionally, he replied in notes to his Home Secretary.

To Churchill, of course, all this was sheer bliss. The more official hats he could wear, the better he liked it. He held the post for only twenty months but they were packed with satisfactions, the sense of power, new experiences, excitement.

The Suffragettes, for example.

Today, the very name has a slightly comic ring. But there was nothing funny about the movement to the English women who were fighting for the vote. They risked their lives, went to prison, endured all manner of indignities for their Cause.

The Churchills drive through Trafalgar Square at the Coronation of King George V, in 1911. That year, Churchill became First Lord of the Admiralty; son Randolph was born.

Cartoons of the period show Churchill, by Max Beerbohm, and as *Punch* satirized his attendance at German military maneuvers, where he met Kaiser Wilhelm II.

The Home Secretary was appointed an Ecclesiastical Commissioner for England in 1911 and leaves Buckingham Palace after a convocation of clergy.

Like the advocates of civil rights today, the Suffragettes demonstrated at public meetings and in the streets. Churchill, being in charge of public safety, became the special object of their wrath. The ladies stormed his office (today no doubt they would have staged sit-ins), and on two occasions he was whacked with riding crops.

On another, a Suffragette said, "I like your moustache as little as your politics."

"Don't worry, Madam," Churchill replied, "you won't come in contact with either."

Far more serious for Churchill was the great strike of transportation workers in 1911. It began with the dock workers who were soon joined by railway employees. When the question of foodstuffs became critical, Churchill attempted to meet it by putting troops on the docks and operating trains. There was gunfire and some strikers were killed.

Was it significant that Churchill kept a bust of Napoleon on his desk?

In any case, he was forced to capitulate. When a settlement was reached, it was Lloyd George, not Churchill, who effected it. The tragic episode may have carried over to 1945 when Labor swept Churchill out of office at the height of his wartime glory.

Having been imprisoned, if only briefly during the Boer War, prison reform interested him greatly. There was much to reform in the penal institutions of the day. Churchill interviewed prison officials and prisoners themselves, studying the problems. He sought information and advice from a friend who had been jailed for a political offense. In *My Early Life,* he showed the effect on him of his own experience:

> I certainly hated every minute of my captivity more than I ever hated any other period of my whole life. Looking back on those days, I have always felt the keenest pity for prisoners and captives. What it must mean for any man, especially an educated man, to be confined for years in a modern convict prison strains my imagination . . . Therefore in after years, when I was Home Secretary and had all the prisons of England in my charge, I did my utmost consistent with public policy to introduce some sort of variety and indulgence into the life of the inmates, to give educated minds books to feed on, to give to all periodical entertainments of some sort to look forward to . . .

Also during this period, in a highly un-British episode, he found an opportunity to indulge his insatiable appetite for danger and excitement.

He was in his bath one morning when his office informed him that a band of Nihilists from the Baltic states, who had shot and killed three unarmed policemen a month before, had been tracked down. After the killings, Churchill issued pistols to the "Bobbies" and to Scotland Yard men assigned to work on the case. Now, the message said, they had trapped the killers in a house on London's East Side. Hundreds of police were firing into the house. Those inside were returning the fire with automatic pistols. Churchill, if any directing of operations were necessary, could have done so from his desk. Instead, he dressed hastily and rushed to the scene. The next day, newspaper photographs showed the Home Secretary, in a top hat, ducking bullets and directing the attack at close range.

Tongues wagged for weeks. Some newspapers found such conduct unbecoming for a Cabinet Minister. In the House, the Tories castigated Churchill as a ridiculous publicity-seeker. (He would hear that charge often repeated in the years ahead.) He himself thought the incident was "great fun."

The Nihilists were not captured. The house caught fire and they died in the flames.

This appears to have been Churchill's first contact with the type of dangerous revolutionaries who were soon to rule Russia. Their objectives in England were not clear. At any rate, Churchill's hostility toward them never left him.

A more immediate enemy, however, now was emerging in Europe.

Several years earlier, Churchill had gone to Germany to witness large-scale Army maneuvers. The Kaiser entertained him royally. An aristocrat and a military man himself, Churchill found the whole experience enjoyable. He admired the Germans' thoroughness and efficiency. The maneuvers, with thousands of infantrymen in spiked helmets precision-marching past the "All-Highest," impressed him.

However, the Germans were rapidly building warships. Here was a clear and present danger to Britain's supremacy on the high seas. Was a naval race developing? Churchill didn't think so. In a debate in the House on the size of Britain's shipbuilding program, he cited "four funda-

Photo from *European*

The First Lord relaxes on the golf links, 1913. Having little talent for the game, he abandoned it early, but continued to shoot and play polo.

mental errors" regarding Germany and said, "The fourth and most fundamental error is that any profound antagonism exists between England and Germany."

Apparently, the "All-Highest" and his courtiers had done a good job of brain washing on Churchill.

Nothing could have been more fallacious than his statement in the House. As the months wore along in 1911, alarming evidence to the contrary rapidly accumulated in London and Paris. In a somewhat ambiguous arrangement, the General Staffs of Britain and France were conferring together. It now appeared that war with Germany might break out at any moment.

In October, Herbert Asquith invited Churchill to play golf in Scotland. The Prime Minister appears to have been thinking for some time about changes in the Admiralty and the War Office. Churchill had some ideas, too. Both men were aware that a time-bomb was ticking on the Continent. But in Scotland they talked about golf and the weather.

Finally, Asquith quietly said, "Would you like to go to the Admiralty?"

"Indeed, I would," Churchill replied.

On October 23, 1911, less than three years before Sarajevo, he entered the Admiralty as First Lord. He would soon be flashing a fateful message to the Fleet.

TRAGEDY WITHOUT TRIUMPH

EVERY DAY IN THE ADMIRALTY, the First Lord made it a point to study the map on the wall of his office. It showed the North Sea. Flags marked the position of the Kaiser's warships. In part, Churchill said later, this was an "act," designed to impress the officers with a sense of urgency. But it was not entirely a gesture. Ten years before, as a very green member of Parliament, young Winston Churchill had stated his belief that the Navy would be Britain's chief fighting arm in the event of war. Now he was its First Lord, responsible for its efficiency, and therefore in his view, for the safety of his country.

His own sense of urgency drove him hard. Who could say how much time remained to get ready for war? As matters turned out, thirty-three months were to elapse between the day he took command of the Admiralty and the fateful chain of events that led to the First World War. Nevertheless, "I intended to prepare for an attack by Germany as if it might come next day," Churchill wrote in *The World Crisis*.

The Admiralty gave full scope for all his dynamism and creative energies. Ideas spewed out of him like lava from volcano. Full steam ahead!

He converted warships from coal-burning to oil, giving them greater range. The 13.5-inch guns on "Dreadnoughts" were replaced with 15-inch guns. How did he know that the ships, designed to mount one weapon, could support the awesome power of bigger guns? He didn't know; he simply took the long gamble. "We acted without ever making a trial gun," he said. "We trusted entirely to the British naval science in marine artillery."

By 1912, another idea was churning around in his restless brain—a naval air arm. Was there a potential military value in the airplane? With Churchill, action generally followed close on the heels of thought. He must know about airplanes. If there is an element of risk in flying today, the chances of a fatal accident were many times greater fifty years ago. Nevertheless, pursuing his research, Churchill made a number of flights. As always, his luck held. It ran out, however, for some of the officers who piloted him. The day after one of his flights, the plane that carried him crashed, killing three men. The British naval air arm came into existence well before military men elsewhere in the world had ceased thinking of the airplane as a toy.

At the same time, Churchill labored to bring about closer liaison between the Admiralty and the War Office. The Admirals and Generals, in effect, worked in air-tight compartments, not as a team. When the question arose of ferrying British troops to the Continent, for example, the brass hats in the two arms advanced totally different views as to what could and should be done. Someone said, as Churchill moved in on this state of affairs, "Winston is knocking over Admirals like ten-pins."

He also butted in on the Army. In a famous memorandum, he calculated that the French Army would be in full retreat by the twenty-first day after fighting began. By the fortieth day, however, he predicted the Germans would be so extended and the French so massed that the situation could be brought into balance. The function of the few British divisions available would be, therefore, to shore up the French left

The Grand Fleet, with H.M.S. *Collingwood,* at Spithead, July 1914.

flank during the critical forty days. A British General called the memo "ridiculous and fantastic."

However, when war broke out in 1914, the pattern developed exactly as foreseen by the First Lord. The French, although committed to the philosophy of the offensive, were unable to sustain their attacks. In three weeks, they were in full retreat. Then, on the forty-first day, the Battle of the Marne opened, bringing a halt to the German advance.

1914

June 28—The Austrian Archduke Francis Ferdinand is assassinated by Serbian nationalists in Sarajevo, Bosnia.

July 18—The British Fleets assemble for review by King George VI. Following the Austrian ultimatum to Serbia, Churchill makes an announcement— "Orders have been given to the First Fleet, which is concentrated at Portland, not to disperse for maneuver leave at present. All vessels of the Second Fleet are remaining at their home positions."

July 28—Austria declares war on Serbia.

July 29—The Imperial Council of Germany decides on war against Russia and France. Churchill issues secret orders for the Fleet to sail, under cover of darkness, to war stations.

August 1—The Government vetoes Churchill's plan to call up naval reservists.

August 2—German troops enter French territory. Churchill, quietly flouting the Government veto, calls the reservists to the colors.

August 4—England, as guarantor of the neutrality of Belgium, declares war when German troops enter Belgian territory. At 11 P.M., Churchill flashes a General Order to the Fleet—"Commence hostilities at once against Germany." At 11:05, the warships are under way.

In the annals of the First World War, it is the records of the German Admiralty that pay Churchill the ultimate tribute. They state that the actions he took between July 18 and August 4 gave England "an extensive military advantage . . . which Germany could not counter nor overtake."

Barely a month later, Churchill's judgment failed him in an operation on land.

On September 28, German artillery opened the attack on Antwerp. The Channel ports were vital to Britain for landing troops and supplies. Field Marshal Horatio Herbert Kitchener, chief of the War Office, said to Churchill, "You must personally dash to Antwerp."

Why Churchill? Kitchener evidently felt that Churchill's brimming energy and electric personality, plus his high position in the Cabinet, would help stiffen Belgian resistance in front of the city. Churchill, always ardent for action and the excitement of war, readily agreed. He was given command of the Royal Naval Division, marines and naval volunteers. Of its 8000 men, only about one-fourth were fully trained. The division lacked rifles. Much of its equipment was obsolete.

The operation was foredoomed. Antwerp fell. Churchill, long before ridiculed by professionals as an "amateur" and "dilettante," came home the scapegoat.

"I ought never to have gone to Antwerp," he said later. "I ought to have remained in London and endeavored to force the Cabinet and Lord Kitchener to take more effective action than they did, while I, all the time, sat in my position of great authority with all the precautions that shield great authority from rough mischance."

Antwerp would return to haunt Churchill. But this was only a bagatelle compared to the real disaster awaiting him.

By 1915, the war had congealed into a defensive stalemate. From Switzerland to the sea, millions of soldiers in trenches peered at each other across the edges of Hell. Hopes faded on both sides for *L'offensive à l'outrance* (all-out attack). Each side kept trying. First, the bombardment lasting for hours. Then waves of infantry struggling through machine gun and rifle fire. They might gain 100 yards, a single line of trenches, or no ground at all. The war of attrition. What to do? More sustained shelling, so great that nothing could live through it, must be the answer.

So the guns must thunder for days, not hours. In the Battle of the Somme, for example, British artillery rained shells on the German positions for a week, day and night, without stopping. Then the Tommies scrambled "over the top," advancing through shredded barbed wire, and the Germans, still miraculously alive and able to fight, scrambled out of their dugouts and mowed them down. Time and again, both sides endured these ghastly ordeals.

In all history, no pattern of war surpassed in horror the war of the trenches, fought from positions on which artillery could be zeroed-in with hairline accuracy, an open field of fire between, defenses all but impregnable to frontal attack. It was a meat grinder.

Out of this grisly deadlock came a new weapon—the tank.

"The trenches must be crushed," Churchill kept saying in the Admiralty.

There were various suggestions out of which the tank finally emerged. Without his incessant pushing and prodding, it might never have come into existence. And had his advice on the use of the new instrument been followed, the breakthrough might have been achieved long before 1918, as will be shown.

The idea was by no means original with any one man. Hannibal had used elephants in battle. Tacticians of many nations had thought of mechanical "elephants." The armored car already was in use.

But no armored car, mounted on wheels, could operate over the tortured terrain in France, spanning shell craters and breaking through barbed wire. Churchill first thought of steam-rollers. Then, it was caterpillar-treads, a system newly developed in the United States.

That fired his imagination. He wrote a letter to the Prime Minister:

"It would be quite easy in a short time to fit up a number of steam tractors with small armored shelters in which men and machine guns could be placed, which would be bulletproof . . . the weight of the machine would destroy all wire entanglements."

The Admiralty developed a model, "Big Willie." Partly for reasons of security, and also because no other name had been found for the awesome creation, it was called a "tank."

On September 15, 1916, out of the grey morning mist at Thiepval, German soldiers saw for the first time what must have looked like primordial monsters lumbering toward them, crunching through their outer defenses.

There was no breakthrough. Only forty-nine tanks went into action and only a few of these

33

Photo from European

A flying enthusiast himself, Churchill, as First Lord, introduced an air arm into the Navy. He is shown in 1914 after completing a flight. He never flew solo, although he often handled the controls himself.

The Gallipoli campaign to force the Black Sea, open the sea lanes to Russia and knock Turkey and Austria out of the war was a costly fiasco and Churchill was the scapegoat. Here Australian and New Zealand troops land at "Anzac Cove" in the Dardanelles.

Radio Times Hulton Picture Library

After the failure of the Dardanelles campaign, Churchill resigned as First Lord of the Admiralty. With Clementine, he addresses a meeting at the Enfield Munitions Works, 1915.

Thirsting for action, Churchill went to France in 1915 as a major with the Grenadier Guards. Wearing a French shrapnel helmet, he stands alongside General Fayolle. "War, which used to be cruel and magnificent," Major Churchill said, "has become cruel and squalid."

reached their objectives. Churchill had counseled delaying until huge fleets of tanks could be launched, striking in numbers while the element of surprise still held.

He was not heeded. By that time, his voice no longer was heard in the war councils.

A year after Thiepval, a tank attack of the dimensions Churchill proposed was launched. Lord Byng of Vimy, the Canadian commander, said, "By 4 P.M., November 20, one of the most astonishing battles in all history had been won."

The effect on the Germans was described by General Erich Von Ludendorff:

"In cases where they have suddenly emerged from smoke clouds in huge numbers, our men have been completely unnerved. They broke through our foremost lines, making a way for their infantry, wrecking our rear and causing panic which entirely upset our control of the battle."

In the Second World War, in which the tank proved such a devastating engine, the British paid Churchill a long-deferred tribute. They named a type of heavy tank "Churchills."

Now back to 1915 . . .

Two developments in the war more or less coincided in that year: the stalemate in France, and Russian appeals for help.

The probability of breaking the deadlock in France began to appear more and more remote, although "Papa" Joffre, Commander-in-Chief of the French, still believed in it. Others, both in Britain and France, cast around for alternative theaters of war. Sir John Fisher, the First Sea Lord—a brilliant, eccentric, imperious commander—proposed to force the Baltic Sea and open a new front in Germany itself. Lloyd George suggested attacking through the Balkans; General Joseph Gallieni, the "savior of Paris," endorsed the idea. There were others.

Churchill now perceived the possibility of attaining both objectives: force the Black Sea, opening sea-lanes for supplying Russia, knock Turkey and Austria out of the war, and thus attack Germany on the flank. He argued for the "back door," just as in the Second World War he proposed striking through the Balkans, the "soft under-belly of the Axis."

The Dardanelles Strait is the key to the Black Sea. Here, at Gallipoli, Churchill aimed what

was to be the master stroke.

Fisher opposed it and so did some French Generals. Churchill's name is indelibly imprinted on the story of this great disaster but others should have shared a degree of responsibility.

For disaster it was.

British and French warships were lost. The attacking infantry never had numerical superiority, much less the customary three-to-one over the defense. Evidently, the fighting qualities of the Turks were not fully appreciated. Not even the magnificent Australian infantry could storm and hold the heights of Gallipoli against such odds. It was a costly failure.

Failure is seldom forgiven in war, regardless of the reason. "I don't like unlucky generals," Napoleon said. Again, as after Antwerp, Churchill became the scapegoat.

Certainly the Australians, after their great effort, did not forgive him. Their official war history said the Dardanelles campaign failed "through Churchill's excess of imagination, a layman's ignorance of artillery, and the fatal powers of young enthusiasm."

Again, the view from the German side is worth noting.

Back in England again, and back in the House of Commons, Churchill takes time off to attend the Chelmsford Fete with Clementine.

David Lloyd George succeeded Asquith as Prime Minister in December 1916. The following year Churchill joined his Government as Minister of Munitions.

The future field marshal (then Lieutenant Colonel), Bernard Montgomery, at left foreground, joins Secretary of State for War Winston Churchill in watching a march-past of the 47th Division as the King of the Belgians re-enters Lille after its liberation, October 28, 1918.

General Erich von Falkenhayn, Chief of the General Staff, said, "If the Straits between the Mediterranean and the Black Sea were not permanently closed to Entente [Allied] traffic, all hopes of a successful course of the war would be very considerably diminished. Russia would have been freed from her significant isolation. . . ."

The operation probably came within an eyelash of success. If the Allies had held on a little longer . . . ? The crux of the question was whether the basic concept was faulty or the manner of its execution. Military historians may never agree.

In the immediate aftermath, Churchill's enemies howled for his head.

He defended himself in a mighty speech in the House. He noted that he had consulted naval authorities on the feasibility of forcing the Dardanelles and that he mapped his strategy partly on the basis of what they told him. The word, "persevere," so often sounded by him in the Second World War, appears frequently in this speech. Nothing he might say could save him.

Clearing out his desk in the Admiralty, he said, "I am finished."

He took up a new hobby—painting. "Painting has been a great solace to me," he said. "It helped me to get over the horrible time after the Admiralty." Today, there are many photographs of the stubby figure, easel in hand, hunched over the canvas, and many Churchill paintings. It all began with the disaster in the Dardanelles.

But no hobby, however engrossing, could hold his interest while the war continued. He wrote Whitehall, "I am an officer and I place myself unreservedly at the disposal of the military authorities, observing that my regiment is in France."

Presently he was in the trenches there. Then he became Colonel Churchill, commanding the Sixth Royal Scots Fusiliers.

The "invisible wings" still beat over him. Once, a shell blew his dugout to bits five minutes after he left it. Again, he went to look for a box of matches and a shell hit the spot where he had been standing.

True or not, there is an anecdote about this period, one of those "bright ornaments" of history, as Churchill called them. Drinking was strictly forbidden at the front. One night, how-

As Britain's representative, Churchill rides with General John G. Pershing, who headed the American Expeditionary Forces, in a victory parade celebrating the end of the war.

ever, Churchill and some officers opened a bottle of wine with their rations. Suddenly, word came down the trench that the commanding General was approaching. An officer quickly snatched up a lighted candle and stuck it in the neck of the bottle. The General chatted for a few moments, wished the officers a good night, and departed.

In London, after the war, Churchill entertained him at dinner. Wine was offered. Eyes twinkling, the General said, "I hope it doesn't taste of wax."

In 1917, Lloyd George made Churchill Minister of Munitions. Then he served as combined Minister for War and Air. He was in his sphere again, busy and happy.

But the downward spiral in his career was beginning. Not long afterward, he became an "out," in every sense of the word.

THE RED FLAG

In the light of his stated fondness for wines and spirits (a quart a day since the age of sixteen?), there is something almost hilarious in the fact that Winston Churchill lost his seat in Parliament to a devout Prohibitionist. His defeat came not on the issue of "drys" versus "wets." It was part of a larger struggle, one that remains to this day.

This was the sequence of events—

After the Great War, Churchill directed British operations in support of the White counter-revolutionaries in Russia. He spoke of the "foul baboonery of Bolshevism." The Bolshevik Revolution, he said, was "an infant that should have been strangled in its crib." He must have been puzzled when the Soviets in 1920 awarded him the Order of the Red Flag for "great work for the international Revolution." Mockery? Or a peculiar Slavic sense of humor?

He hoped then to be appointed Chancellor of the Exchequer. The office, which had been held by his father, implies leadership of the House and stands on the main line to the Prime Ministership. Lloyd George passed him over and made him head of the Colonial Office.

In 1906, he had been Under-Secretary in this office. It was no great advance after fifteen years.

However, as usual, he made his contributions. He established a Middle East Section and the man who came to be known as Lawrence of Arabia pays him a terse, astringent compliment for it in *The Seven Pillars of Wisdom*. Churchill also played a major role in the settlement of Britain's difficulties with Ireland. He passed along this incident in his negotiations with Michael Collins, one of the Irish leaders:

"He [Collins] was in one of his most difficult moods," Churchill wrote, "full of reproaches and defiances, and it was very easy for everyone to lose his temper.

" 'You hunted me day and night,' he exclaimed. 'You put a price on my head.'

" 'Wait a minute,' I said. 'You are not the only one.' And I took from my wall the framed copy of the reward offered for my recapture by the Boers. 'At any rate, it was a good price—£5000. Look at me—£25 dead or alive. How would you like that?'

"He broke into a hearty laugh . . . all his irritation vanished."

Then came the 1922 election.

At that time, Dundee sometimes was called, justly or otherwise, "The drunkenest city in Scotland." One of its residents was a gentleman who rejoiced under the name, E. Scrymgeour. He was a teetotaler and therefore conspicuous in Dundee. Over a period of years, he had conducted twin crusades, to dry up the city, and to unseat its representative in Parliament, Winston Churchill.

Five times, Mr. Scrymgeour contested Churchill's seat and lost. In 1922, he succeeded.

It was the first time since 1900, and the only time in a total of sixty-four years, that a Churchill was not a member of the House.

What brought about the defeat?

Socialism was the rising new force in Britain after the Great War. Economic depression and unemployment fostered its growth. There was peace at last, but nothing resembling prosperity for the working classes. The Government appeared incapable of taking effective remedial

As Secretary of State for War, Churchill inspects British troops stationed in Germany, 1918.

In 1924 Churchill stood for Parliament as an Independent anti-socialist candidate in the Abbey Division of Westminster. He was defeated by 43 votes. The following October he was the successful Conservative candidate for the Epping Division.

As Chancellor of the Exchequer (June, 1927), Churchill drives to 10 Downing Street with Prime Minister Stanley Baldwin to discuss the coal crisis.

The year 1929 saw the death both of three-year-old Marigold, the Churchill's third daughter, and of Winston's mother. Diana, their first child, was born in 1909; Sarah in 1914. A year after Marigold's death, Mrs. Churchill gave birth to a fourth daughter, Mary.

still weak and in some pain when he rose to make his one speech before the election.

A frightening scene immediately developed. Waves of hostility, beyond anything he had ever encountered, greeted Churchill.

In a British election campaign, the candidate usually must contend with a certain amount of heckling, questions shouted at him, some serious, some merely for the sake of heckling. In Dundee, the tumult reached a point where it drowned out Churchill's temporarily feeble voice. Had he been allowed to speak, he would have urged a line of policy running midway between the demands of the Socialists and the position of the Government. But he was not allowed to speak.

Someone began singing "The Red Flag" and others joined. Churchill stepped down.

When the election returns came in, Churchill found himself badly beaten. "I have no office, no Party, no seat, and no appendix," he said. Adversity, to him, was something that could be met with a wisecrack.

He tried again in two other districts. Again, virulent hostility. It appeared to be organized, duplicating the demonstration in Dundee. "Antwerp . . . Antwerp," someone would shout. Others would cry out, "What about the Dardanelles?" This had no relation to political issues or the economic problems. It was personal and it appeared to Churchill to be a "campaign of defamation." He hit back—

"In the whole of the findings of the Report of the Royal Commission, there is not one word of detraction of what I did. Don't imagine I run away from the Dardanelles. I glory in it."

It became necessary for him to go to political meetings with a police escort. His wife, attempting to relieve him of some of the burden of campaigning, scheduled a speech in a strongly Socialist district. The police warned her against appearing there.

Churchill failed in both tries. The British people now banished him to private life. His political stock was at rock bottom.

steps. A newspaper cartoon of the day showed a line of shabbily dressed men, standing in a drenching rain, looking for work. The very image of misery and despair. One says it all reminds him of Flanders and the War. "But at least we had a job then," the other replies.

Communist influences may have been at work. But the larger scene was that which developed in the United States during the Great Depression and takes the form today of "Liberal" versus "Conservative" philosophies.

Churchill, says Lewis Broad in *Winston Churchill*, regarded Socialism "as only a shade less detestable than the virulence of Bolshevism." He had broken with the Liberals by that time and, calling himself a Free Trade, went into the campaign of 1922.

Before he could begin, he was stricken with appendicitis. Surgery was performed. He was

41

FPG

In 1923, he brought out the first volume of his history of the Great War, *The World Crisis.* A typical remark about him during this period was, "Churchill has written a long book about himself and called it *The World Crisis.*"

He used the royalties, $100,000, to buy a country home in Kent, Chartwell Manor. There he now went to live. He would stay in bed until about noon every day, reading and answering correspondence. In the afternoon, he painted or indulged another hobby, laying bricks. He built some new walls on the grounds. Not all his work shows a highly professional skill. Nevertheless, when word of his encroachment in the field reached the Brick Layers Union, questions were raised about the non-union threat in Kent. Churchill took out a union card and paid his dues regularly.

Inevitably, he returned to politics.

In 1924, now calling himself a "Constitutionalist," Churchill campaigned for a seat in the House of Commons as the representative for Epping.

He had made such a mark and become so much a fixture of the House that even a newspaper that had opposed him said he was "incomparably the best man in the field . . . his presence was badly required in the House of Commons." Churchill received powerful support from some Tories, one of whom informed him, "The old quarrels of Liberal and Conservative belong to the past."

He was returned to the House and remained there for 40 years until his retirement in 1964.

In 1925, Churchill returned to the Conservatives. Stanley Baldwin, the Prime Minister, appointed him Chancellor of the Exchequer, the steppingstone office to becoming the King's First Minister.

His functions did not directly concern development of new weapons but he says that in 1925, he wrote:

> May there not be methods of using explosive energy incomparably more intense than anything heretofore discovered? Might not a bomb no bigger than an orange be found to possess a secret power to destroy a whole block of buildings—nay, to concentrate the force of 1000 tons of cordite and blast a township at a stroke?
>
> Could not explosives even of the existing type be guided automatically in flying machines by wireless or other rays, without a human pilot, in ceaseless procession upon a hostile city, arsenal, camp or dockyard?

This was twenty years before Hiroshima and before the German V-weapons crashed down on London. In the same passage, he also foresaw germ warfare. Poison gas, of course, had been used in World War I, but he said ". . . only the first chapter had been written of a terrible book."

All this is either a remarkable example of clairvoyance, or else Churchill had been talking with scientists. The possibility of splitting the atom was not new. Experiments in rocketry had been going on for years. He does not say how these thoughts came to him.

An accomplished bricklayer, Churchill (shown with daughter Sarah), built this house at Westerham in 1930, was accepted as a member of the Amalgamated Union of Building Trade Workers.

The versatile Chancellor of the Exchequer began painting in his forties, sold his first painting in 1934. Much of his spare time in the 1920's was also spent writing his monumental volumes on World War I as well as other books.

The General Election of 1929 returned the Labour Party to office and signalled Churchill's decade-long political eclipse. He is shown on the way to the House of Commons to deliver his last budget speech, with his wife, daughter Sarah and son Randolph.

A few months after losing political office, Churchill was installed as Chancellor of the University of Bristol.

At any rate, they made a deep impression on him. No wonder he was so alert to developments that could lead to a Second World War and tried so hard to rouse his countrymen when, in the next decade, he did perceive the signs in the skies over Germany.

Churchill remained in Government until 1929. Then, once again, he was on the outside. It seems doubtful that he could have abandoned the dream of being Prime Minister, but nevertheless he said, "I have cheerfully and gladly put out of my mind all idea of public office."

As he stepped down from office, a decade ended. The 1920's seem unimaginably distant, not in time but from the standpoint of change.

Serious efforts at disarmament followed "the war to end war." Naval ratios were established. Battleships were sunk. The Treaty of Versailles barred the door to German rearming and the signatories to the Kellogg-Briand Pact pledged themselves not to resort to war. The term, "Dictator," belonged largely to Roman history.

In Italy, Mussolini was making the trains run on time. In Germany, Jewish war veterans saluted the significant dates of the Great War along with any other ex-soldier. In Japan, civilian authority predominated; its leaders were not interested in military adventures in China or anywhere else.

As for the United States, no serious domestic or foreign problems troubled Washington in 1929. Two chickens in every pot . . . two cars in every garage. With a little luck, you could make a million in the Stock Market and keep most of it. It was the Age of Innocence. There was a song, "Runnin' wild . . . I've lost control."

All this was swept away soon after the 1920's ended. The shadows quickly rose. "Runnin' wild . . . I've lost control." The words were more prophetic than anyone could know.

"SHALL WE ALL COMMIT SUICIDE?"

Throughout the 1930's, as the Dictators rose and the evil era began, Winston Churchill held no office in Government. He was an "outcast," as Edward VIII said. His only function was to play Cassandra to successive British Governments. Yet nothing could have been more fortunate for him in the long run, and for Britain and the Western democracies.

He remained in Parliament. Thus he had access to a forum in the spotlight, a platform from which he could plead, warn and protest. But having no official position, he bore none of the onus for the indecisive policies followed by Britain—and the other democracies—before the Second World War. No stigma of "appeasement" could be attached to his name; on the contrary, he never ceased to rail against the ill-starred concessions to the Dictators. If, by 1939, Nazi Germany was armed to the teeth, Churchill in no degree could be held responsible; year after year, he sounded the alarm, reporting the growth of German military might. In 1936, he said, "Dictators ride to and fro upon tigers which they dare not dismount. And the tigers are getting hungry."

The peculiar fate of Cassandra was that she possessed the gift of prophecy, but her prophecies were not believed. Neither were Churchill's. But at least he had uttered them. They were on record. So he would well say:

"This was not the first time—or indeed the last—that I have received a blessing in what at the time was a very effective disguise. Now one can see how lucky I was. Over me beat the invisible wings."

Churchill went out of office in 1929 and for ten years his services went begging. When he was recalled, in 1939, it was to be First Lord of the Admiralty, the scene of his first eclipse.

He settled down to the life of a country squire at Chartwell. "I built with my own hands a large part of two cottages and extensive kitchen-garden walls," he said, "and made all kinds of rockeries and waterworks and a large swimming pool which was filtered to limpidity and could be heated to supplement our fickle sunshine. Thus I never had a dull or idle moment from morning to midnight, and with my happy family around me dwelt at peace within my habitation."

In 1931, he came to the United States for a lecture tour. British lecturers were almost inordinately popular with American audiences then and of course Churchill was better known than most.

He was on his way to see his friend, Bernard Baruch, in New York one night when he was nearly killed on Fifth Avenue. Forgetting that traffic in Britain and the United States moves on opposite sides of the road, he stepped out into the path of a speeding taxi. "For two months I was a wreck," he said.

The lecture tour went off successfully. He found Americans "cool and critical but also urbane and good natured . . . on the whole I found it easy to make friends with American audiences." Chicago was an exception. In that city, he said, "I encountered vocal opposition." Shades of Big Bill Thompson, the Mayor, who was supposed to have said, "If King George ever comes to Chicago, I'll punch him in the nose!"

During this period, Churchill also completed the biography of his great ancestor, the Duke of

Charlie Chaplin was a guest at Chartwell, Churchill's home at Westerham, Kent, in 1931. Two years earlier Churchill had visited Chaplin in Hollywood.

Marlborough. In researching for the book, he went to Germany in 1932, studying Marlborough's battlefields. At the same time, he found out all he could about the Nazi movement and its leader, a strange, wild-eyed man called Adolf Hitler.

One day, a man whom Churchill believed acted as emissary for Hitler made contact with him in Munich on a purely social basis. He said he could easily arrange a meeting between Churchill and Hitler.

Churchill agreed. He asked a number of questions about Hitler, among them, "Why is your chief so violent about the Jews?" He said he saw no reason for condemning a man because of the circumstances of his birth. Probably because of this, the interview never took place. "Thus, Hitler lost his only chance of meeting me," Churchill said.

Early in the Thirties, the shadows began lengthening across the world: The economic depression, the time-bombs built in to the Treaty of Versailles, growing nationalism, the spirit of revenge, lust for power—these and many other factors began dragging the Great Powers toward the brink.

After a swim at Deauville, he sought to hide from public view, with the assistance of the Duke of Sutherland.

A skeletonized chronology to show the sequence of events follows:

1930—Economic depression in the United States with serious depressive effects in Europe and Japan.

1931—Japanese attack Manchuria; Henry L. Stimson, U.S. Secretary of State, fails to organize collective opposition.

1932—A Japanese puppet state, "Manchuokuo," is set up.

1933—Adolf Hitler becomes Chancellor of the Reich.

1934—Hitler, now in complete power, repudiates the clauses of the Versailles Treaty prohibiting German rearmament.

1935—Mussolini attacks Ethiopia; a policy of economic sanctions "short of war" fails.

1936—The Rome-Berlin "Axis" is proclaimed; German troops reenter the Rhineland; the Spanish Civil War begins and becomes a testing ground for modern weapons.

1937—Japan attacks North China; Franklin D. Roosevelt warns the aggressors in the "Quarantine Speech."

1938—The Munich Agreement; Hitler annexes Austria.

1939—Dismemberment of Czechoslovakia; Non-Aggression Treaty between Hitler and Stalin; Hitler attacks Poland beginning World War II.

1940—Japan and Germany join in a Treaty of Mutual Assistance; first Japanese moves into French Indo-China.

On a 1931 speaking tour, Churchill was struck down by a taxi in New York City while on the way to visit his old friend Bernard Baruch. Before lapsing into semi-consciousness he managed to say to the driver: "It's all my fault." He leaves the hospital three weeks later.

A chipper Churchill leaves a nursing home after a severe attack of paratyphoid in 1932.

Thus, Germany, Japan and Italy came together against the democracies. All were dictatorships. In Japan, no single man held that position; a group of military leaders succeeded in elbowing aside the civilian authorities. Seeing the success of Hitler and Mussolini in territorial aggrandizement, the Japanese openly eyed territory in China.

They began separately but by the end of the 1930's they were united in a program of piracy. Japan's warlords began it.

Churchill was extraordinarily perceptive but he was not omniscient. Writing about the Japanese seizure of Manchuria, he said he could not blame the British Government if "they did not seek a prominent role at the side of the United States in the Far East without any hope of corresponding American support in Europe." Yet British interests in the Orient, especially in China, were many times greater than those of the United States.

Again, when Mussolini attacked Ethiopia in 1935, Churchill merely said:

"I speak as a proved friend of Italy and I must express surprise that so great a man and so wise a ruler as Mussolini should be so willing and even so eager to put his gallant nation into such an uncomfortable military and financial position."

So great a man and so wise a ruler! A few years later, Churchill was calling Mussolini "a whipped jackal."

He supported the British Government's policy of non-intervention in the Spanish Civil War, too. "It is at Geneva [the League of Nations] rather than in Spain that the peace of the world may be best secured," he said.

Churchill added in the same speech, "Meanwhile, let us press forward with our rearmament for the world danger grows."

He kept his eyes fixed primarily on the Nazis. He had his own private channels of information from Germany, and they seem to have served him well. As early as 1932, he said in Parliament:

"I have the greatest respect and admiration for the Germans and the greatest desire that we should live on terms of goodwill and fruitful relations with them. But I put it to the House that every concession that has been made . . . has been followed by a fresh demand."

Great efforts had been made earlier in Washington, London, Paris and Tokyo to bring about substantial disarmament. But early in the

1930's, Churchill counseled a different course. He said:

"The bringing about of anything like equality of armament while grievances are unredressed will appoint the day for another European war." He cited Danzig, the Polish Corridor and other transfers of territory sanctioned by the Allies after World War I. Churchill continued:

"The road of pressing for disarmament leads us deeper into the European situation. The removal of grievances removes the cause of danger or leads us out of danger itself."

It is profitless to speculate as to whether Hitler would have been stopped if Churchill's advice had been followed. But at least, the Fuehrer would have been deprived of some of his most effective screaming-points when his hour came.

Not long after the Nazis completed the seizure of power in Germany, one man recognized that Churchill—although he held no official position—was a threat to their future plans. He was the crafty dwarf, Joseph Goebbels, Minister of Propaganda. He said:

> For years now, Churchill has painted not landscapes but a picture of the German danger. He is the leader of the implacable haters of Germany in England . . . he sets in motion those waves of gall which are not to be taken light-heartedly. His disposition for untenable accusations, Muenchausen fairy tales and polemics dates presumably from the time he was correspondent of the *Daily Telegraph*.

Goebbels was a clever man. Even as the skies darkened in the 1930's, there were those in the democracies who clung to the belief that "we can-do-business-with-Hitler." Such men would be only too ready to believe that Churchill's warnings were "fairy tales."

Now came, unrelated to the mainstream of events, a painful episode for Churchill. In 1936, King Edward VIII let it be known that he intended to marry a slim, dark-haired American, Mrs. Wallis Warfield Simpson, of Baltimore. She was a divorcée. The Prime Minister, Cabinet, Parliament and probably a majority of the British people were opposed. Beneath a self-imposed silence in the British newspapers, this great conflict rushed toward a climax. The King had few allies.

American-born Wallis Warfield Simpson became the bride of the Duke of Windsor in 1937 following his renunciation of the throne and the title King Edward VIII. Churchill, who supported Edward, helped him to write his farewell address.

Churchill aligned himself with the King. Here again, you find him championing an unpopular cause, regardless of the political consequences. In 1900, it had been the plea for a policy of magnanimity toward the Boers. Now it was an issue much more highly charged with emotion. "I have never repented of this," Churchill said, "indeed, I could do no other."

Churchill was a monarchist. He cherished it as an institution, and he was steeped in the history of relations between Crown and Parliament. After he abdicated and became Duke of Windsor, the King wrote in his memoirs:

"When Mr. Baldwin had talked to me about the Monarchy, it had seemed a dry and lifeless thing. But when Mr. Churchill spoke, it lived, it grew, it became suffused with light."

Churchill wrote Baldwin a famous letter, "I plead for time and patience." He argued that, since Mrs. Simpson's divorce was not yet final, no Constitutional question existed in fact between the King and Parliament. To gain time was his first objective, and then if possible, to find a way out of the impasse. The letter had no effect. The Duke said in his memoirs:

> Although my advisors and I realized there was nothing to be gained by prolonging the unequal contest, Mr. Churchill at this late

During the 1930's the future Prime Minister wrote his massive and majestic biography of his famous ancestor the first Duke of Marlborough.

hour still insisted that more remained to be said . . . He strode into the House of Commons on the Monday afternoon, undaunted and quite alone, to launch his attack.

Hardly was he on his feet before the hostility smote him like a great wave. The memorable scene of Mr. Churchill being howled down has often been described . . .

Churchill's own version—

"There were several moments when I seemed to be entirely alone against a wrathful House of Commons. I am not, when in action, unduly affected by hostile currents of feeling; but it was on more than one occasion almost physically impossible to make myself heard."

The King abdicated. Churchill's part in the case resulted in driving his political stock still further down. The Duke wrote that Churchill now became a political "outcast." Churchill himself said ". . . it was the almost universal view that my political life was at last ended."

Nevertheless, he persisted in what he considered the main task, to prod the Government into action while there was yet time. In another of his symmetrical sentences, he accused the Government of being "decided only to be undecided, resolved to be irresolute, adamant for drift, solid for fluidity, all-powerful to be impotent." In a heated moment, he cried out in the House, "Shall we all commit suicide?"

Munich, in 1938, was the next-to-last act in the fateful chain of events.

Under pressure from Britain and France, Czechoslovakia ceded the Sudetenland to Hitler. Militarily, Churchill said, this was equivalent to adding twenty-five infantry divisions to the German Army. Apart from that, he said, "The idea that safety can be purchased by throwing a small state to the wolves is a delusion."

Then one of the most memorable of all his lines—"All is over. Silent, mournful, abandoned, broken, Czechoslovakia recedes into the darkness. She has suffered in every respect by her association with the Western Democracies and with the League of Nations, of which she has always been an obedient servant."

He reproached the Government for "five years of futile good intentions, five years of eager search for the line of least resistance."

Munich probably delayed the war in Europe by twelve months. But it was the Nazis who profited most from the time gained. On August 22, 1939, Joachim von Ribbentrop and Vyaschislav Mikhailovich Molotov, toasting each other with sparkling champagne, signed a treaty. It was short, only seven articles, the first of which said:

"The two contracting parties undertake to refrain from any act of force, any aggressive act, and any attacks against each other, under-

On September 1, 1939, Hitler invaded Poland. On the 3rd, England and France declared war on Germany. That evening Churchill was suddenly called by the Government to resume his old post as First Lord of the Admiralty. He walked into Parliament that evening to a standing ovation.

taken either singly or in conjunction with any other powers."

In less than two years, Hitler tore up that "scrap of paper." With his eastern flank now secure, he allowed only eight days to elapse before attacking Poland, on September 1, 1939.

Armageddon was at hand.

Two days later, honoring her alliance with Poland, Britain declared war on Germany. The French followed suit.

Neville Chamberlain, the Prime Minister, formed a War Cabinet. He asked Churchill to return to the Admiralty as First Lord. Churchill accepted. Here he was, back in the same office he had occupied in 1915, with the same North Sea maps and the memories of the Dardanelles.

When he took up his duties again, a message was flashed to the Fleet, "Winston is back."

Every bearded British tar knew what it meant, and this is one of the finest of all the tributes paid Churchill.

He was nearly sixty-five years old, but for him this was the beginning of the prime of life.

Viscount Norwich later wrote, "It is hardly too much to say that if he had died in 1939 at the age of sixty-five, he would have been recorded as one of those brilliant failures whose names litter the pages of history and are soon forgotten."

At that point, it is true, Churchill had failed in his two primary efforts, to be Prime Minister, and to rouse Britain's leaders to the danger of the Dictators.

But now, at long last, he neared his own finest hour. In less than a year, he would be leading Britain as the Prime Minister.

51

THE BULLDOG

He would stand before the House of Commons, jaw jutting, feet planted wide apart, a short, barrel-bodied figure, solid as Gibraltar. Generally, he wore a dark suit, vest, a wing collar and a perky bow tie. As he spoke, he occasionally tugged at the lapels of his jacket. His lower lip stuck out pugnaciously. To Grandmother Jerome, he had looked like a "naughty little sandy-haired bulldog." Only a few wisps of grey hair now remained, but the bulldog look was more pronounced than ever. A throaty note would thicken his voice when he growled some fresh defiance at Adolf Hitler, "We will have no truce or parley with you or the grisly gang who work your wicked will. You do your worst—and we will do our best."

He had an exquisite sense of timing, equal to a comedian's. He used it to point up the gibes with which he leavened his grimmest oral reports on the war. During the period, 1940-41, when Britain faced the Nazis alone, he said, "We are still awaiting the promised invasion." He paused. Utter stillness filled the House of Commons. Then he added, matter-of-factly, "So are the fishes."

A storm of laughter swept the crowded benches and echoed across all of Britain.

This was Winston Churchill in the graveyard days of the war, whistling his loudest. He was an emotional powerhouse, a galvanizing force, steeling his countrymen to the ordeals ahead, assuring them that some day, somehow, on some as yet unimaginable battlefield, the awesome power of Germany would lie in ruins. "The day will come when the joy bells will ring again throughout Europe and when victorious nations . . . will plan and build in justice, in tradition and in freedom . . ."

At the time, one could only say of this man, "Whom the gods would destroy they first make mad."

He began his wartime leadership with the naked and now-famous, "I have nothing to offer but blood, toil, tears and sweat." He cribbed this from one of his own books, a passage he had written about the plight of Russian troops in 1917, "Their sweat, their tears, their blood bedewed the endless plain."

Addressed to a people who often say, "I prefer to know just where I stand," it was a shrewd beginning.

And Dunquerque was a favorable augur, a foretaste.

By any criteria, the evacuation was a brilliant operation. When it began no one could say how many British troops might be snatched from the jaws of the German trap, perhaps 50,000 at the most. In fact, 338,226 men were ferried to England. The nation rejoiced. Churchill, however, told Parliament in a famous speech, "We must be very careful not to assign to this deliverance attributes of a victory. Wars are not won by evacuations . . ."

Upon learning of the large number of troops rescued, he said later, his first impulse was to organize a counterattack. However, so much equipment had been abandoned in France that this was impossible. Instead, he bent himself to the task of exhorting the British to stand firm as Hitler's forces coiled for invasion.

In her book, *Mr. Churchill's Secretary*, Elizabeth Nel pictures him composing the speeches

that not only roused the British but stand among his greatest contributions to the final victory four years later—

On these occasions he would walk up and down the room, his forehead crinkled in thought, the cords of his dressing-gown trailing behind him (he often wore his favorite red, green and gold dressing-gown when dictating). Sometimes he would fling himself for a moment into a chair; sometimes he would pause to light a cigar, which with so much concentration was neglected and frequently went out. For minutes he might walk up and down trying out sentences to himself. Sometimes his voice would become thick with emotion, and occasionally a tear would run down his cheek. As inspiration came to him he would gesture with his hands, just as one knew he would be doing when he delivered his speech, and the sentences would roll out with so much feeling that one died with the soldiers, toiled with the workers, hated the enemy, strained for Victory.

Miss Nel wrote that Churchill dictated from 1 A.M. until 4:30 in preparing one speech. "During this particular session," she writes, "he stopped once to ask if I were tired, and when I told him I was not, he said, 'We must go on and on like the gun-horses, till we drop.'"

The words still ring, majestic rolling periods, like the tones of Big Ben in London—

Do not let us speak of darker days. Let us speak rather of sterner days. These are not dark days; these are great days—the greatest our country has ever lived; and we must all thank God that we have been allowed, each of us according to our stations, to play a part in making these days memorable in the history of our race.

Even though large tracts of Europe and many old famous states have fallen, or may fall, into the grip of the Gestapo and all the odious apparatus of Nazi rule, we shall not flag nor fail, we shall go on to the end.

We shall defend our island whatever the cost may be. We shall fight on the beaches, we shall fight on the landing grounds, we shall fight in the fields and in the streets, we shall fight in the hills, we shall never surrender.

(True or not, people were delighted with the story that Churchill, still panting from this long passage, then gasped, "and if need be, we shall bash their heads with bottles.")

You ask what is our policy? I say it is to wage war by land, sea and air, war with all our might and with all the strength that God has given us . . . You ask what is our aim? I can answer in one word. It is victory.

If we can stand up to him [Hitler], all Europe will be free . . . Let us therefore brace ourselves to our duty, and so bear ourselves that if the British Commonwealth and Empire last for 1000 years, men will still say, "This was their finest hour."

After the war, Churchill tended to minimize his role in steeling the British to go on fighting, to hope when no reason for hope could be seen ahead, to endure the losses in life and property.

"I have never accepted what many people have kindly said, namely that I inspired the nation," he said.

"It was the nation and the race dwelling all 'round the globe that had the lion's heart. I had the luck to be called upon to give the roar. I also hope that I sometimes suggested to the lion the right place to use his claws."

In some degree, he may have been right in thinking this. It is difficult to believe that any

As First Lord of the Admiralty, in February, 1939, Churchill addressed the men of the *Exeter* which had taken part in the destruction of the German pocket battleship *Graf Spee* off Montevideo, Uruguay.

Neville Chamberlain continued as Prime Minister during the first eight months of the war, resigned on May 10, 1940, as Hitler invaded the Low Countries. That night King George VI called Churchill to Buckingham Palace and named him Prime Minister.

The new Prime Minister leaves 10 Downing Street in May 1940 with two members of his war cabinet, Sir Kingsley Wood, Chancellor of the Exchequer (left), and Anthony Eden, War Secretary.

St. Paul's Cathedral is visible through a heavy pall of smoke after an air raid on London during the Blitz in 1940. Below: smoke from the burning docks drifts over London Bridge.

Frenchman, for example, endowed with all of Churchill's dynamism and powers of inspiration, could have roused the French to continue fighting after the German breakthrough.

Meanwhile, along with all this speech-making, Churchill was fighting a war, directing and supervising the thousand-and-one principal operations of a government at war. The range of his concerns was gigantic. Yet, he also busied himself with minute details—

What! British fighter pilots carried only 50 francs in their fighter sweeps over France? "In my view, at least 3000 francs should be carried as part of a pilot's equipment, and passed from hand to hand."

Newspapers reported a court martial in which a sergeant cussed out a lieutenant in the presence of troops but was merely reprimanded. "He surely should have been reduced to the ranks," the Prime Minister's memo said.

"Let me have a short note showing the number of boys who leave the public elementary schools at fifteen years and over . . . I am anxious that the educational and disciplinary aspects of these boys' lives shall rank as prominently in our minds as the need to find considerable numbers for A.R.P., A.A. batteries, et cetera."

He discovers that the female members of a mixed anti-aircraft battery "have been deprived of badges, lanyards, etc., of which they were very proud. Considering that they share the risks and the work of the battery in fact, there can be no justification for denying them incorporation in form."

Amid your many successes in your difficult field, the egg distribution system seems to be an exception. I hear complaints from many quarters and the scarcity of eggs is palpable . . . Will you please give me a very short statement of your plans and policy.

I see reports in the papers that timber-felling companies are ruthlessly denuding for profit many of our woodlands . . . Let me know in a few lines what you are doing to replant.

I shall be glad to know what action you have taken about enabling the twelve couples of married internees to be confined together.

Pray do this . . . Pray let me have by noon today. . . .

When the Prime Minister surveyed the ruins of the House of Commons in 1941 he was moved to tears and declared, "This Chamber must be rebuilt—just as it was. Meanwhile we shall not miss a single day's debate through this!"

His concern for detail irritated Field Marshal Earl Wavell, according to the four senior officers who wrote *The Mediterranean and the Middle East,* an official war history. Churchill deluged Wavell with telegrams and the book says:

"Although they were typical of Mr. Churchill's normal methods, these telegrams contained so many inquiries and suggestions about matters of detail well within the province of a commander-in-chief that to General Wavell, . . . they were irritating and, in his opinion, needless."

The daily blizzard of memos originated, for the most part, in Churchill's bedroom. He stayed in bed until nearly noon, dictating and reading reports. After lunch, he napped for an hour or so. Then he would work on until 2 A.M. or later, often with a Scotch-and-soda at his elbow.

He thrived on the heavy burden, even gaining weight. "Clemmie" worried and urged him to eat less. He agreed. The new regimen lasted exactly seven hours, that is, through one day's lunch until dinner time.

To travel outside Britain, of course, was dangerous but he journeyed hundreds of thousands of miles, by sea and air, especially during and after 1941 when the Axis Powers brought Russia and the United States into the war.

In North Africa, Churchill had a severe attack of pneumonia, with heart complications. His temperature rose to 102, the pulse rate was 130, his heart fluttered, and a bluish cast came into his face. His doctor, Lord Moran, feared blood clotting might set in.

Flying him to Morocco from Tunis, some 1,200 miles, a dispute developed between the pilot, Air Vice Marshal Thomas K. Kelly and Lord Moran. The physician said Churchill could not be taken above 3,000 feet. Kelly felt that, by administering oxygen, it would be safe to fly higher. Bad weather developed. Churchill himself settled the dispute.

"If I were not in this aircraft," he said, "it would be flying at 19,000 feet. It is ridiculous keeping it so low, and it will crash into the mountains." Turning to his daughter, Sarah, he said, "It is my wish, but I do not give it as an order, that the captain fly higher." Using the oxygen, Kelly climbed to 20,000 feet. Churchill, with his usual tact, thanked both Kelly and Lord Moran when he recovered. "You thought of everything," he said.

The incident is related in Kelly's diary which he published after the war.

This tremendous strain, long hours of work, other bouts of illness and frequent travels, took place during the five war years when Churchill's age advanced from sixty-five to seventy. He seemed indestructible.

As in the First World War, some of Churchill's pet military projects turned out badly. His zeal for the offensive may have caused two operations to have been launched prematurely, in Norway in 1940 and in Greece in 1941. Capt. Stephen W. Roskill wrote in the official British history of the war at sea:

> It does seem that one result was that they delayed and impeded the transition from the defensive to the strategic offensive.
>
> We may at least be thankful that the expedition to the Baltic which Mr. Churchill so strenuously urged in 1939-40 was overtaken by events and that other premature offensives, such as the proposed attack on Pantelleria and the Dodecanese in 1940, never took place.

These setbacks (and Dieppe was still to come) seem never to have discouraged Churchill nor to have shaken his faith in ultimate victory. Thus, he refused to accept anything short of total victory when the opportunity presented itself.

In 1940, two months after Churchill became Prime Minister, Hitler, in effect, offered peace. He said:

"I consider myself in a position to make this appeal since I am not a vanquished foe, begging favors, but the victor speaking in the name of reason. I can see no reason why this war need go on . . . It grieves me . . . Possibly, Mr. Churchill will brush aside this statement of mine . . ."

Mr. Churchill could hardly wait to brush it aside, "We will have no truce or parley with you . . ."

The bold front concealed a truly desperate condition in Britain. Churchill later revealed just how desperate, "We had not at that time fifty tanks. We had a couple hundred field guns, *some of them brought out of museums.*" (Italics ours.) Another man, considering the threat of invasion in the light of this weakness, might have found it the better part of valor to accept a truce, peace without victory. The bulldog, having begun to fight, would not let go.

So, in preparation for invasion, Hitler began the saturation bombings . . . London . . . Coventry . . . Bristol . . . Liverpool . . . Manchester . . . Cardiff . . . many cities. The world had never seen such a rain of incendiaries and high explosives.

Night after night, the air-raid siren wailed. (Some musical genius had pitched it to a note that struck terror in your heart before the first bomb fell!) Anti-aircraft batteries opened up. Over London, it was like a "blitz" in reverse, as much going up as came down. Then the bombs. Meanwhile, British fighter pilots were taking a terrible toll of German planes, inflicting such losses that the Luftwaffe never could gain command of the air. The Battle of Britain.

Bright and early in the mornings after the big raids, Churchill went out inspecting the damage. He often wore his "siren suit," a kind of coveralls he designed himself. He clambered over the debris, king-sized cigar at a jaunty angle, flashing his V-sign, talking with the victims. There were shouts, "Good old Winnie," and then tears often filled his eyes. General Dwight D. Eisenhower, in his wartime memoirs, said, ". . . he never ceased to show great concern for my safety, although paying absolutely no attention to his own. His single apparent desire, during an air raid, was to visit his daughter, Mary, then serving in an anti-aircraft battery protecting London."

Churchill reported to the House on one such inspection tour.

I was asked last week whether I was aware of some uneasiness, which it was said, existed in the country on account of the gravity, as it was described, of the war situation . . . And I went to some of our great cities and seaports which have been most heavily bombed, to some of the places where the poorest people have got it worst.

I have come back not only reassured but refreshed . . . it is no hackneyed figure of speech to say that they mean to conquer or die.

So they held on through 1940, passing through what Churchill called "this scowling valley" of time. An Englishman, rising from his desk on a Friday night, said to an American, "Well, here's another weekend coming up and Jerry still hasn't invaded. One often wonders whether there will be another weekend."

Winter weather and the angry Channel waters all but ended the danger of invasion for 1940.

Then 1941, and a great turning-point: On June 22, a Sunday, Hitler attacked the Soviet Union. Britain no longer stood alone.

What was Churchill's position? For more than twenty years, he had been known as an "arch anti-Communist." Now the Russians were ranged beside Britain against Germany. Churchill's secretary asked if it embarrassed him to have the Reds as allies?

"If Hitler invaded Hell," Churchill replied, "I would make at least a favorable reference to the Devil in the House of Commons."

Churchill, the morale booster, waved his hat on a stick while touring a provincial town that had suffered the attentions of the Luftwaffe.

Throughout the Battle of Britain Churchill made it his custom to inspect bombing damage. Here he looks over a small hotel in Ramsgate wrecked a few hours earlier in an air raid.

Franklin Roosevelt and Churchill met off Newfoundland aboard the *Augusta* on August 14, 1941 and issued a joint declaration of peace aims which came to be known as the Atlantic Charter.

Casablanca, in French Morocco, was the rendezvous of Churchill and Roosevelt in January 1943. Here they worked out plans for an Allied offensive designed to secure the unconditional surrender of Germany.

That night, broadcasting to Britain and the world, he said:

> The Nazi regime is indistinguishable from the worst features of Communism. It is devoid of all theme and principle except appetite and racial domination. . . . No one has been a more consistent opponent of Communism than I have for the last twenty-five years.
>
> But all this fades away before the spectacle which is now unfolding. The past, with its crimes, its follies and tragedies, flashes away.

Then the heart of the message, "Any man or state who fights on against Nazidom will have our aid . . . It follows therefore that we shall give whatever help we can to Russia and the Russian people."

He established contact with Stalin as soon as possible and a British mission went to Moscow, curious to see how they would be received. A possibly apocryphal story, another of those "bright ornaments" of history, came out at the time—

A Russian officer, so it went, took a British officer on a sightseeing tour in Moscow. "This," he said, "is Churchill Boulevard, formerly Hitler Street." They came to another thoroughfare. "This," said the Russian, "is Eden Avenue, formerly Ribbentrop Street." He opened a cigarette case. "Will you have a cigarette?"

"Thank you, Comrade, formerly Bastard," said the Briton.

Very soon, the Russians began pressuring Churchill to open a "second front" in Europe to draw off the weight of the German drive across a broad front in Russia. Coincidentally, if it was a coincidence, posters blossomed all over London, "Open the Second Front NOW." The hard military facts of life were, however, that the initial German successes in Russia were so decisive that Hitler might soon be in a position to concentrate anew for the invasion of Britain. Churchill said as much in the House of Commons. Commenting on this, the former German staff officer, General Walter Warlimont, says in his book, *Inside Hitler's Headquarters,* "This shows that the Head of the British Government was clearly reckoning upon an early victory for Germany in the East and that, like Hitler, he also looked upon the German advance into Russia as a way around via the back door to the *coup de grâce* against England."

In these circumstances, Churchill could hardly entertain the idea of opening a "second front." The Russians, however, demanded it even more strongly. Churchill says the Russian Ambassador, Ivan Maisky, at last adopted a tone of "menace" in their discussions of the matter and he says he shot back:

"Remember that only four months ago we in this island did not know whether you were not coming in against us on the German side. Indeed, we thought it quite likely that you would. Even then, we felt sure that we should win in the end. We never thought our survival was dependent on your action either way."

The German legions rolled on, irresistibly, in the first months of the war in the East. These successes now set in motion a chain of events on the other side of the world.

The warlords of Japan, already dazzled by the German victories in the West, now became virtually convinced that Hitler would soon win the war. He had given them a green light, so far as

On a visit to the Southern Coast of England, Churchill inspects a crack unit of Commandos. He is examining the knife of one of the men.

In his "semi-naval" uniform, he signs his autograph for an admiring schoolboy while visiting a port.

The "Former Naval Person" receives good wishes of sailors and airmen as he disembarks from the *Queen Mary* which brought him home from his fifth conference in the United States with President Roosevelt. He replies with his famous "V"-for-Victory sign.

In June 1943 Churchill flew to General Dwight D. Eisenhower's headquarters in Algiers to discuss the plans for the invasion of Italy. From left to right are Anthony Eden, General Sir Alan Brooke, Air Chief Marshal Tedder, Churchill, Admiral Sir Andrew Cunningham, General H. R. L. Alexander, General George Marshall, General Eisenhower, and General Sir Bernard Montgomery.

At the Quebec conference in August 1943, Churchill, President Roosevelt, and Canadian Prime Minister MacKenzie King conferred on the opening of a second front in Europe. Shown with them is the Earl of Athlone, Governor General of Canada.

On his way to the three-power conference at Cairo in November 1943, Churchill stopped at the Island of Malta. Here he inspects the destruction of the dockside area.

At Cairo, the Prime Minister held talks with Roosevelt and Generalissimo Chiang Kai-Shek, President of the Chinese Republic. They announced their joint determination to reduce Japan to surrender. In the back row, left to right, are: General Chang Chen, Lieutenant General Ling Wei, Lieutenant General B. B. Somervell, Lieutenant General Joseph Stilwell, General H. H. Arnold, Field Marshal Sir John Dill, Admiral Lord Louis Mountbatten and Major General Carton de Wiart. Madame Chiang is seated at right.

Teheran, in Iran, was the scene of another three-power conference immediately after the Cairo meeting. The conferees concerted their war plans and reached agreement on the scope and timing of operations.

After the Teheran meeting Churchill suffered a severe bout with pneumonia and spent several days recovering at Eisenhower's villa in Carthage. He wears a colorful dressing gown over his famous siren suit.

When a new carbine was issued to American troops in March, 1944 for use in the coming invasion of Europe, Churchill joined Eisenhower and General Omar Bradley in trying it out. Both generals were amazed at his marksmanship.

A month before V-E day the Prime Minister visited troops preparing for the initial landings in Normandy. Accompanying him is General Montgomery.

In August, with the invasion well under way, Churchill visits General Bradley near the front.

Touring the battle areas in an armoured car, the Old Soldier witnessed heavy shell fire. On one occasion a shell burst within 50 yards of him.

On the Italian Front in late August 1944, Churchill watched a British Army artillery shoot near Florence. He autographed one of the shells. Later, while shells burst in the target area as he watched through binoculars, he remarked, "This is rather like sending a rude letter and being there when it arrives."

On November 11, 1944, Churchill visited Paris and, with General Charles De Gaulle, paid homage to the French Unknown Soldier during Armistice Day ceremonies.

the British, French and Dutch colonies in Southeast Asia were concerned. The Far Eastern Red Army, one of Stalin's best, no longer posed the same threat to Japan. Moreover, the Nazis, while aiming to avoid war with the United States for the time being, sought to induce Japan to make some move that would divert American attention from Europe.

So the moment seemed ripe to the Japanese militarists to seize what Tokyo newspapers were openly calling the "golden opportunity." There was much talk of the "Southeast Asia Co-Prosperity Sphere." If they could achieve it without American intervention, so much the better. (That was the purpose of the efforts of Nomura and Kurusu to negotiate an agreement with Franklin Roosevelt in the dying months of 1941.) If not . . .

The Japanese eventually did for Churchill what he had been unable to do for himself— bring the United States into the war against the Axis Powers.

Roosevelt, as was clear from the first, wanted war with the Nazis. The problem for him was American public opinion. American sympathies were with Britain. But sympathy and the willingness to see American blood spilled in Europe were two different things. Sympathy, except in the case of some individuals who joined up in Canada, did not extend that far. Roosevelt himself had said in the 1940 Presidential campaign, "I have said this before, but I shall say it again and again and again: Your boys are not going to be sent into any foreign wars." Congress passed the extension of the Selective Service Act by one vote! Since a Congressman presumably knows 67

As the war in Europe began to draw to a close, Churchill, Roosevelt and Stalin gathered for a conference at Yalta in the Crimea. Together they concerted their plans for the final defeat of Germany and for the occupation and control of the defeated country.

The Prime Minister gleefully extends his greetings on a 9.2 shell before it is fired into a German position during a visit to Germany in March 1945.

On March 25 Churchill crossed the Rhine with General Montgomery in an American landing craft. A month later Franklin Roosevelt was to die, providing him with his worst moment of the war. Final victory over the Germans was only a few weeks away.

what the folks back home are thinking, this would indicate half the people were opposed to getting into the war.

So the position was difficult, as Churchill well knew. Roosevelt could only edge closer to the brink with "methods short of war" . . . Lend-Lease . . . the deal with Churchill for fifty American destroyers . . . naval patrols in the Atlantic . . . finally, the Atlantic Conference.

On December 7, 1941, Pearl Harbor changed everything. In *The Grand Alliance*, Churchill tells us his feelings when he heard the news—

"No American will think it wrong of me if I proclaim that to have the United States at our side was to me the greatest joy . . . So we had won after all! Yes, after Dunkirk, after the fall of France . . . after seventeen months of lonely fighting and nineteen months of my responsibility in dire stress, we had won the war!"

Hitler declared war. General Warlimont says he was instructed to advise where American forces might first be employed, in Europe or the Far East. He says he replied ". . . so far we have never even considered a war against the United States and so have no data on which to base this examination; we can therefore hardly undertake the job just like that."

In less than a year, the tide definitely turned. The British mauled Rommel's Afrika Korps at El Alamein, opening the way to the liberation of all North Africa and the Russians scooped up a huge German Army at Stalingrad, and the German retreat began.

Thus, by January, 1943, after the Casablanca Conference, the Allies began considering the terms for ending the war, and they told Hitler and the world what they would be, "unconditional surrender."

Shortly after the Conference, Churchill again narrowly escaped death. A bomb hit the Treasury, next to Number 10 Downing Street, and killed twelve persons. Churchill and some aides were at dinner. The blast next door brought a huge chandelier crashing down on the table in front of him.

After the war, too, a macabre secret was revealed. Churchill, when he traveled by sea, prepared for his death in the event of imminent capture. He carried a pistol himself, and an officer was ordered to shoot him if something prevented him from killing himself.

Finally, after the Allied advances through Sicily, Italy and Southern France (Churchill opposed the latter move), the moment came for D-Day and the Normandy hedgerows.

Churchill secretly arranged to sail over and watch the landings but his secret leaked. Came a note from the King:

> My Dear Winston:
> I am a younger man than you. I am a sailor and as King I am the head of all these services. Is it fair that you should do exactly what I should have liked to do myself?
> You said yesterday afternoon it would be a fine thing for the King to lead his troops into battle as in the old days. If the King cannot do this, it does not seem right that his Prime Minister should take his place.

Piqued and disappointed, Churchill wrote back:

"Since Your Majesty does me the honor to be so much concerned about my safety on this occasion, I must defer to Your Majesty's wishes and indeed commands . . . though I regret that I cannot go."

In another year, Hitler was dead, Allied and Russian armies were rushing toward each other from opposite sides of Germany, and German commanders signed the armistice at Reims, France.

"A splendid moment in our great history and our small lives," Churchill said.

Even as he tasted the heady wine of victory in Europe, a rude shock was taking shape for him at home.

"THE LAST PRIZE"

THE GREAT YEARS OF WINSTON Churchill's life constitute the history of a Forty Years War. He waged it against two enemies: German militarism and Communist expansionism. The conflict extended from 1914, when the First World War began, through the Second World War, and until 1955, when he resigned in his second term as Prime Minister. He himself regarded these four decades as an almost uninterrupted struggle against the two forms of tyranny. He equated them in the words, "The Nazi regime is indistinguishable from the worst features of Communism." Immediately after World War I, Churchill sent British troops into Russia to fight the new-born Bolshevik movement. Even before the end of World War II, he foresaw conflict with the Russians and the beginning of the Cold War. Only a few deceptively quiet periods appeared during this long span of time.

Early in 1945, victory in Europe was in sight. The war with Japan could not last much longer, once the Allies concentrated their forces in the Pacific. Churchill began worrying about Russia's postwar intentions. He addressed a number of messages to Presidents Roosevelt and Truman on the question. "Surely it is vital now to come to an understanding with Russia," he said. Here again he was the Cassandra of the 1930's.

The future position of Berlin particularly concerned him. He felt strongly that the city should be captured by American and British forces and not by the Russians. On April 1, 1945, he said in a long message to Roosevelt:

If they [the Russians] take Berlin will not their impression that they have been the overwhelming contributor to our common victory be unduly imprinted in their minds, and may this not lead them into a mood which will raise grave and formidable difficulties in the future? I therefore consider that from a political standpoint we should march as far east into Germany as possible, and that should Berlin be in our grasp, we should certainly take it. This also seems sound on military grounds.

In later years, the Russians did indeed seize on the theme of "overwhelming contributor," glorifying the role of the Red Army in the war and picturing the Anglo-American operations as peripheral skirmishes for the most part.

Churchill also urged on General Eisenhower that "we should shake hands with the Russians as far to the east as possible," referring to the approaching juncture of the Allied and Soviet Armies in Germany.

Later, Churchill sadly recorded, "Actually, though I did not realize it, the President's health was now so feeble that it was General [George C.] Marshall [Chief of Staff] who had to deal with these grave questions."

Another participant, Robert Murphy, says in his book, *Diplomat Among Warriors:*

But Roosevelt was in no condition . . . to offer balanced judgments upon the great questions of war and peace which had concerned him for so long. His conversations illumined for me why the Army during this period was

In the same stirring tones with which he had inspired his countrymen during the darkest days of the war, Churchill addressed them by radio on V-E Day, May 8, 1945. "This is your victory," he said, "victory in the cause of freedom in every land. In all our long history we have never seen a greater day than this . . . Long live the cause of freedom. God save the King."

making decisions which the civilian authority for our Government normally would have made. . . . The situation demonstrates a weakness in our government structure despite our superb Constitution.

In other words, Berlin was a *political* matter of supreme importance but Churchill's views on the question were not reaching Roosevelt. So, against Churchill's counsel, the Russians were permitted to capture and isolate Berlin. Within three years, this monstrously unnatural situation brought the Berlin Blockade and military crisis that might have exploded into war. Clemenceau might have been referring to the sad facts of Berlin when he said, "War is too important to be left to the Generals."

Roosevelt died April 12, 1945. One month later, Churchill sent a message to Truman saying, "Like you I feel deep anxiety" about the Russians. He pointed out what he called Soviet "misinterpretations" of the Yalta agreements. In this message he used a phrase which endured and became common property in other languages. "An iron curtain," he said, "is drawn drown upon their front. We do not know what is going on behind." Thereafter, the Iron Curtain, written in capital letters, symbolized the demarcation line between the Communist world and the West.

The mistrust of course was mutual. Stalin had not forgotten Churchill's role in the 1919 Allied operations against the Bolsheviks.

On May 7, 1945, the Germans surrendered at Reims, France. Allied war correspondents who witnessed the frigid ceremony were advised, however, that the news would not be released for the time being. Imagine blanketing under censorship the most transcendently important event in six years! No immediate explanation was given. Later, it appeared that the reason

On V-E Day Churchill joined the Royal Family on a balcony at Buckingham Palace to acknowledge the cheers of celebrants. Shown from left are the future queen, then Princess Elizabeth; Queen Mother Elizabeth; then Queen; Churchill; the late King George VI, and Princess Margaret. **Wide World Photos**

for this grotesquerie was that a surrender ceremony was to be held in Berlin, May 9. Edward Kennedy, chief of the Associated Press staff on the Continent, refused to comply with the blackout. He notified the military censors in Paris that he intended to release his report of the Armistice, found a channel, and smuggled out the story on the same day.

If Kennedy had not defied censorship, the surrender, so far as the world knew, would have taken place under Russian auspices in Berlin, giving them a maximum propaganda coup. Truman was a novice in foreign affairs at the time. Churchill was not, but he never explained why he consented to the unhappy arrangement.

In July, Churchill, Truman and Stalin met at Potsdam. Robert Murphy's memoirs give this picture of Churchill at the conference:

> During the earlier sessions, Churchill had disappointed his admirers by making a poor showing in some verbal exchanges with Stalin. Sometimes he got facts and figures wrong, sometimes he presented illogical or unconvincing arguments at wearying length. The President had been noticeably restless during some of the Prime Minister's more repetitious speeches. Stalin, however, although relentless in argument with Churchill, had been surprisingly patient in listening to him.
>
> Everybody understood that Churchill was under tremendous strain when he arrived at Potsdam.

Indeed he was. A General Election had been held in Britain but nobody knew the results. Churchill probably was thinking more about the Election than post-war patterns on the Continent.

It had been held July 5 but the votes were not to be counted until July 25. The interval, nerve-wracking to all the principals, was necessary to collect the huge absentee vote from British troops spread around the world. The election could have been delayed until autumn. Moreover, the Japanese were still fighting with suicidal frenzy. But the Conservative Party strategists evidently felt that this was the opportune moment for the election, while Churchill's towering prestige was at the zenith and the "joy bells" of victory still echoed in Britain.

Keystone

At the Potsdam conference in July 1945, Churchill joins Marshal Stalin and the new American President Truman in a triple handshake. During the conference the Labor Party triumphed in a General Election. Churchill was replaced as Prime Minister by Clement Attlee.

Churchill left Potsdam to receive the results. Each set of returns brought a shock, political earthquakes that left Churchill's Government in ruins. When the dust settled, Labor held 393 seats in the House of Commons to the Conservatives' 197.

What happened? Why did the British turn out of office the man who had led them through five thunderous years, through the days of defeat to   73 the moment of victory? Many factors affected the election. For one thing, the Laborites knew pretty well what they wanted in the country after the war, whereas the Conservatives, during the campaign, offered little that was concise or new.

Even during the war years, Labor had been formulating policy. Once, while I was talking politics in London with a Labor M.P. at that time, he startled me by saying, "When this war is over, we're going to turn out the whole Tory crowd, including Churchill." I remember suggesting that this would take some doing if Churchill's prestige and popularity remained as high as it was then. He replied, confidently, "You'll see."

And so it was.

Churchill, flashing his V-sign, said, "The decision of the British people has been recorded in the votes counted today. I have therefore laid down the charge which was placed upon me in darker times. I regret that I have not been permitted to finish the work against Japan. For this, however, all plans and preparations have been made . . ."

Plutarch observed, "Ingratitude toward their great men is the mark of strong peoples."

In any case, it was a great stroke of luck for the Russians. Roosevelt and Churchill, who had dealt with Stalin for four years, no longer sat at the conference table. Who can say how the course of the Cold War, already beginning, would have run if these two had been present to oppose Stalin instead of Truman and Churchill's successor, Clement Attlee?

Churchill was nearly seventy-one when he got the sack. Certainly, he had earned a rest. But he abhorred inactivity as Nature abhors a vacuum. One of his Scotland Yard bodyguards, Walter H. Thompson, said ". . . with nothing to do he is a kicker of wastebaskets." When he heard speculation that he would now retire, Churchill snorted, "I have no intention of retiring in an ardor of civic honors."

While at the Potsdam conference Churchill inspected the ruins of Hitler's Reichschancellery.

Out of power again, the former Prime Minister visited President Truman in March 1946, journeyed to Westminster College in Fulton, Missouri, to deliver his historic "Iron Curtain" speech warning of the Russian threat and calling for unity of the Western world.

In this period, too, it was suggested that he be knighted for his great services in the war. Churchill wryly retorted, "How can I accept the Order of the Garter from my Sovereign when his people have just given me the Order of the Boot?"

Later, however, he did accept a knighthood and in the sunset of his years became Sir Winston.

He packed his papers, returned to Chartwell and set to work on his monumental history of the Second World War. As the theme for the first volume, he wrote, "How the English-speaking peoples through their unwisdom, carelessness and good nature allowed the wicked to rearm." If this seems to exculpate all other peoples it is only a restatement of Churchill's belief that Britain and the United States, standing together, can frustrate the forces of tyranny in the world.

Now, as leader of His Majesty's Loyal Opposition, he plunged furiously into Parliamentary battle. He damned the Socialists and all their works with a cutting weapon, ridicule. "The queues are longer, faces are longer, the shelves are barer, but nevertheless the conduct of daily life is more exacting." He liked Clement Attlee personally, but he said the Prime Minister "is a modest man—he has much to be modest about."

During one of his long speeches, he paused to drink a glass of water. As he put down the glass, he said, thoughtfully, "I don't often do that." The M.P.'s, knowing his habits, roared with laughter.

While still in office, he had said, "I have not become the King's First Minister in order to preside over the liquidation of the British Empire." Now he inveighed fiercely against policies that resulted in independence for India, Burma and Malaya. He would not, or could not, accept the fact that the Colonial Age had ended after 400 years.

In a summing-up speech, he said, "Our Oriental Empire has been liquidated, our resources 75 have been squandered, the pound sterling is worth only three-quarters of what it was when Mr. Attlee took over from me. Our influence among the nations is now less than it has ever been in any period since I remember."

His personal influence, however, remained enormous, even though he was out of office, as was demonstrated in 1946 at Fulton, Missouri.

He went there to receive an honorary degree from Westminster College. Then he delivered the famous "Fulton Speech." In it, Churchill sounded the first clear warning from any major statesman in the world regarding Soviet intentions. He used his "iron curtain" analogy again. He prefaced it by saying:

> I have a strong admiration and regard for the valiant Russian people and for my wartime comrade, Marshal Stalin. . . . We welcome constant, frequent and growing contacts between the Russian people and our own people. . . . It is my duty, however, to place before you certain facts about the present position in Europe.

Then he exploded the bomb heard round the world:

> From Stettin in the Baltic to Trieste in the Adriatic, an iron curtain has descended across the Continent. Behind that line lie all the capitals of the ancient states of Central and Eastern Europe.
>
> I do not believe Soviet Russia desires war. What they desire are the fruits of war and the indefinite expansion of their power and doctrines.
>
> In a great number of countries, far from the Russian frontiers and throughout the world, Communist Fifth Columns are established and work in complete unity and absolute obedience to the directions they receive from the Communist center.

He proposed an alliance between the United States and Britain as the foundation-stone for a unified Western Europe. Later, many other men would say that the Russians could be dealt with only from a "posture of strength." Churchill said at Fulton:

"I am convinced there is nothing they admire so much as strength, and there is nothing for which they have less respect than military weakness."

A favorite Churchillian form of relaxation during his relatively quiet years was riding. Here he participates in a hunt at Chartwell Farm, 1948.

Today, all this is a twice-told story . . . Soviet ambitions . . . subversion by Fifth Columns, the necessity for negotiating from a "posture of strength."

But in 1946, the man on the street knew little or nothing about the course the Soviets were

The unity of Europe was an ideal for which Churchill worked arduously in the postwar years. Here he addresses a meeting of the Council of Europe at the Hague in 1948, and reviews a detachment of French infantry at Strasbourg during another Council meeting in 1949.
Wide World Photos

pursuing. Only a year had passed since the end of the war when the Russians were allies. Photographs of G.I.'s shaking hands with Russian infantrymen on the Elbe were still fresh in memory. American officials who had dealt with Stalin and his aides during the war had long since shed any illusions about continued cooperation with Russia after the fighting ended. The Soviets had been co-belligerents with the West against a common enemy, but their post-war designs were not those of Churchill and Roosevelt. Few people realized that.

And so a tremendous uproar swept the world after Churchill's speech. In both the American Congress and the House of Commons there were expressions of shock and deep disapproval. It seems incredible that a United States Senator or a British M.P. could have been so badly informed in 1946, but many were. Stalin called Churchill a "war monger," and termed the Fulton Speech "a dangerous act." Churchill had blown the whistle on him.

At the same time, the speech undoubtedly alerted some men in policy-making positions, even though at first they did not agree with his conclusions.

Events soon vindicated his warning.

The Soviet grip tightened over Eastern Europe, Poland, Hungary, Czechoslovakia. A high Czech official, Jan Masaryk, son of the great Czech patriot, plunged through a window to his death. Was it murder or suicide to escape Com-

Back in harness again was Winston Churchill in 1951 when the Tories were narrowly victorious in a General Election, bringing him back to the Prime Ministership for the second time, at the age of 77.

Churchill became the first Commoner ever to be installed as Lord Warden of the Cinque Ports, which provided him with a hat and ceremonial dress resembling an admiral's uniform with cuffs and collar heavily ornamented in gold.

munist torture? Red guerrillas attacked the frontiers of Greece. Political and economic strife, engineered by local Communist parties, wracked France and Italy. In 1948, the Russians made the boldest of all their moves in this period—the Berlin Blockade. The blockade was circumvented by the Allied Airlift after a year. But there were many who felt that this should have provided the reason for a showdown, especially since the United States already had the A-bomb then and the Russians did not. Probably the lack of American resolution then encouraged the Communists to take the next step, outright war in Korea in 1950.

Churchill, meanwhile, was concentrating his energies on the plan he had broached at Fulton, organizing a United Europe. In the course of this, he offered two thoughts which seemed novel and unlikely, if not impossible—that France and Germany, enemies for centuries, must now come into partnership, and that a rearmed Germany was essential for the defense of Europe. Here again, as in the Fulton Speech, he was several years ahead of his time and not, as some critics thought, totally cockeyed.

All the while, at more or less regular intervals, the succeeding volumes of his war history appeared. To help him write them, aides and secretaries plowed through the mountains of his personal papers, messages, speeches, the thousand-and-one memos on every conceivable subject. He organized the material and dictated his comments and explanatory asides. Then he revised by hand, again and again.

One day, while he was thus engaged, a lady came to call on Mrs. Churchill. While they were chatting, her small son slipped away and managed to find Churchill's study. He watched, wide-eyed for a moment, and said, "They say you are the greatest man in the world. Are you?"

"Yes," Churchill garrumphed. "Now get out of here."

In 1950, the Conservatives again lost in the General Elections. The margin, however, was narrow, unlike the crushing defeat in 1945. Another election came in 1951.

Churchill, nearly seventy-seven now, campaigned tirelessly. Of course, he enjoyed few activities more than campaigning and this no doubt made it possible for him to be on the stump day after day at his age.

On the eve of the election, standing bareheaded on a hillside, he said:

> If I remain in public life at this juncture it is because, rightly or wrongly, but sincerely, I believe I may be able to make an important contribution to the prevention of a Third World War, and to bringing nearer that lasting peace settlement which the masses of the people of every race and in every land fervently desire.
>
> I pray indeed that I may have this opportunity. It is the last prize I seek to win.

When the returns were counted, he found himself again in harness, the harness he liked best.

Crowds gathered outside Buckingham Palace when he drove up in answer to the King's summons. He was twirling a gold-headed cane, beaming, puffing the inevitable up-tilted cigar. The people called out "Good old Winnie," as in the war days. He grinned and responded with his V-sign. In the Palace, the King and Churchill went through the formalities for the second time. How different from the first summons, when neither man knew whether he would even be able to remain in Britain much longer!

Soon the floods of memos again flowed from the Prime Minister's office to all branches of government, each bearing some familiar Churchillian hallmark such as, "Pray let me know by noon today . . ."

A few good years remained to Churchill.

THE TURNING POINT

At QUESTION-TIME IN THE HOUSE of Commons, the galleries, press seats, and the diplomats' section would be completely filled. No matter how many times you saw Winston Churchill in action, it was always an experience. Around 3 P.M., the Prime Minister would appear, lumber slowly to the Government front bench, and ease his bulky frame into his seat. He wore the same costume as in the war years, black jacket, grey trousers, vest and bow tie, but with one innovation now, zippers instead of laces on his shoes.

Question-time is like a Presidential press conference in Washington, except that M.P.'s ask the questions and frequently the Prime Minister has received notice in writing that such-and-such a point will be raised. His aides dig out the facts and he frames the answers. On these occasions, both in Washington and London, not all the questions are models of intelligence, nor framed in the fewest number of words. You sometimes get the impression that the questioner has risen merely to be seen on television, or in the House, to get his name in Hansard, the official record of the proceedings. Churchill, like John F. Kennedy, was a master in the art of skewering inanities.

A Member, at about this time, asked Churchill what plans had been made for transferring the Government away from London in the event of war. The Prime Minister replied, "You must not expect me to take the bread out of the mouths of the Russian secret service."

After question-time, he would go to his office to read reports or meet with members of his party. Or he might stroll into the smoking room of the House where, traditionally, the youngest M.P. is entitled to chat informally with a Prime Minister.

He drank Scotch before dinner, white wine with the main course (whatever it might be), and cognac afterward.

Even during his second term, when Britain was not at war, Churchill usually worked nights. He liked to play *bezique,* a card game similar to pinochle. It is said that during a game he would often call in a secretary, ask about some report, or whether So-and-so had been advised of something Churchill wanted done. The dispatch cases containing official business never were far from him no matter where he went.

Some years earlier, Churchill acquired another hobby, owning and racing horses. His first, Colonist II, was purchased in 1949 for $5,600. Colonist II won 13 races and $36,000 in prize money. The horse, like his master, refused to run to his left. Churchill liked that.

These years were among the happiest of his life. He was in his seventies but still in good health. He enjoyed his avocations, painting, bricklaying, playing the kettledrums, butterflies, goldfish and race horses. Even more, he enjoyed the dueling in the House of Commons and the power and responsibilities of his office. He once said, "Power, for the sake of lording it over fellow creatures or adding to personal pomp, is rightly judged base. But power in a national crisis, when a man believes he knows what orders should be given, is a blessing." Strictly speaking, no "national crisis" confronted Britain in Churchill's second term as Prime Minister. He was, however, acutely concerned with the Cold War and the long-range objectives of the Soviet Union.

A happy boy catches the Prime Minister for an auto-graph. Mrs. Churchill stands behind her husband.

During a trip to Venice, the Churchills enjoy a dip at the Lido Beach.

As his American grandfather and his father before him, Churchill took up racing after the war. He is shown with his first horse, Colonist II, which had just won the Winston Churchill Stakes at Hurst Park, May 1951.

More than an amateur painter now, Churchill was in every respect a successful artist. His works commanded good prices and some were hung in London's Royal Academy. Above left, he works on an oil during a holiday in Madiera. Below: *Le Beguinage, Bruges* (1946). Above right, the Brazilian Ambassador to London holds a Churchill painting he has just purchased.

Chartwell, Churchill's house in Kent which he built in the Twenties from royalties on *The World Crisis,* was opened to the public in May 1952 to raise funds for the YWCA, of which Churchill was vice president.

Gathered at Chartwell are the elder Churchills surrounded by some of their family. At left are Duncan Sandys, Mrs. Sandys (Diana Churchill); sitting cross-legged is their son Julian. Emma Soames (daughter of Mary Churchill) perches on her grandfather's knee, while her brother Nicholas occupies a cushion. Seated next to Grandfather is Winston, son of Randolph Churchill, who stands at right. His daughter Arabella cuddles beside Mrs. Churchill.

Paul Popper, Ltd.

During one of his several visits to his old school, students cheer Harrow's most famous "old boy."

Churchill visited the United States in January 1952 and addressed a joint session of Congress for the third time in his career.

Wide World Photo

In 1952, for the eleventh time, he came to the United States. And for the third time, he addressed a joint session of Congress. Among the points in his review of the uneasy peace in the world, he described "the new unity growing up in Europe." It resulted of course from the Soviet menace. Churchill said he believed this drawing-together process would continue, and if so, "the architects in the Kremlin may be found to have built a far better world structure than they had planned." (Vice versa, when "peaceful co-existence" became the Soviet line, and a slight thaw developed in the Cold War, cracks and seams appeared in Western unity.)

On this trip, Churchill became a member of the Society of Cincinnati, an organization of Americans who had fought in the Revolution. He qualified through one of his mother's forebears, Lieutenant Reuben Murray, of the Connecticut Continentals. Churchill fingered the insignia of the Society, hung around his neck, and said, "When the events took place which this Society commemorates, I was on both sides of the war between us and we."

In March, 1953, Josef Stalin died. Georgi Maximilianovitch Malenkov succeeded him. Could this open the way for a change in Soviet policy, a relaxation of some of the tensions in the world? Churchill, as a result of his wartime experiences, believed firmly in sitting down at the conference table with the heads of other states to settle joint problems.

Moreover, Churchill's old friend, "Ike," as he called him, was now in the White House. They had worked closely together during the war. Eisenhower said they had had some fierce arguments, which he attributed to Churchill's American blood—"he just couldn't stop talking." But they remained on close personal terms. Churchill now indirectly proposed that another "Sum-

In the course of his American trip, the Prime Minister attended a reception given in his honor by Secretary of State Dean Acheson. He is shown with his daughter, Sarah Churchill (left), and Margaret Truman. British Information Servic[e]

mit" with Malenkov might be fruitful. Planning began for a preliminary meeting with Eisenhower in Bermuda.

Meanwhile, on June 2, Elizabeth II was crowned.

Her Coronation in Westminster Abbey was a majestic ceremony, gleaming with dress uniforms, diamond tiaras, heavy fur robes, coats-of-arms, a scene of medieval pageantry. When the Ladies, acting on cue, removed their tiaras with arms encased in shoulder-length white gloves, they looked like a flock of startled swans. Set patterns prescribed the actions of each person participating in the rites, from which he was not to depart by jot or tittle.

Not Churchill. He came waddling up the aisle with the Prime Ministers of the Commonwealth countries. He wore a thick fur robe. The costume, draping his bulky frame, made him look like a tank. By protocol, members of the Diplomatic Corps, Lords and Ladies, and others had been seated in the Abbey before the Prime Ministers.

As they entered the Abbey, walking at a slow wedding-march step, Churchill caught sight of General George C. Marshall, the President's personal representative, sitting in a front pew. He stepped out of the procession, walked over to Marshall and shook hands with him. Then he resumed his place in the group. Eyebrows raised. There was a slight gasp. A Lady, struggling to suppress a giggle, covered her mouth with her hand.

(Rules seldom were for Churchill. On one of his tours of the United States he lodged in the staid old University Club in New York. Members say that, one morning, he strolled through the lobby in pajamas and dressing gown, entered the reading room overlooking Fifth Avenue, and sipped a brandy and soda there while reading the morning papers.)

As one who cherished the Monarchy, the Coronation was an hour of glory for him. Over the B.B.C. that night, he spoke of the young Queen as "the lady whom we respect because she is our Queen and whom we love because she is herself." The deep voice that so often growled and rasped in a speech was vibrant with emotion during the broadcast. It was a great and joyous time for Churchill.

Not many more remained to him.

A few weeks later, it was announced that the Bermuda Conference had been postponed. No precise reason was given. Then the word came that the Prime Minister's physicians had advised him to rest after a siege of particularly heavy work.

The truth was that he had had a stroke.

Actually, it was the second stroke. The first, in 1950, had been light. The second was serious. It paralyzed his left side and rendered him unable to speak. He was seventy-nine years old. At that age, the effects of such an attack are generally irreversible. Brendan Bracken, his Minister of Information during the war, gave him a wheelchair equipped with chromium-plated ap-

On a visit to New York in January 1953 he relaxed with Bernard Baruch, his friend since World War I, and President-elect Dwight D. Eisenhower.

The December 1953 conference in Bermuda, where Churchill poses with Eisenhower and French Premier Joseph Laniel, had been postponed because, it was announced, Churchill was required to rest from overwork. Later it was revealed that he had had a stroke, his second.

pliances to make life more pleasant. At first, they amused and interested Churchill. Then it seems to have occurred to him that he was dependent on buttons and gadgets to get around. He managed to convey to "Clemmie" and Lord Moran that he wanted to work. State papers were brought to him. Officials called. His indomitable will would not permit him to remain an invalid. Slowly, he overcame the paralysis. In October, he could and did make a speech.

Then he attended the Bermuda Conference with Eisenhower and Joseph Laniel, then Premier of France. Little of importance came out of it but Churchill called the talks "encouraging." With Anthony Eden, his Foreign Secretary, he saw Eisenhower in Washington again in 1954.

However, not much official life was left to the old lion. On his eightieth birthday, he said, "I am now nearing the end of my journey."

More honors came to him. Queen Elizabeth knighted him in 1953 and in the same year he received the Nobel Prize for Literature.

Churchill was unable to accept it in person. Lady Churchill represented him. She smiled when a Nobel committeeman said, "The Nobel literary prize is intended to cast lustre over the author, but this time it is the author who gives lustre to the prize."

She then accepted the diploma, medal and a check for $33,840 from King Gustav. Next, Lady Churchill read his message:

The Nobel Prize for Literature is an honor for me alike unique and unexpected and I grieve that my duties have not allowed me to receive it myself here in Stockholm from the hands of His Majesty.

I am proud but also, I must admit, awe-struck at your decision to include me. I do hope you are right. I feel we are both running a considerable risk and that I do not deserve it. But I shall have no misgivings if you have none.

Since Alfred Nobel died in 1896 we have entered an age of storm and tragedy . . .

Radio Times Hulton Picture Library

Honors continued to be heaped upon Churchill. In 1953 he was knighted by the Queen, and in the same year he received the Nobel Prize for Literature. On June 14, 1954 he was formally installed as a Knight Companion of the Most Honorable and Noble Order of the Garter (right), at a service held in St. George's Chapel, Windsor. Below, he is on his way to the installation. The Queen Mother talks to the Duke of Gloucester, while Churchill, in his Garter robes, is at left.

Keystone Press

Sir Winston in his role as public speaker and Parliamentarian lost none of his vigor or eloquence as his 80th year approached. Here he addresses a mass meeting of Conservative women in 1954.

On Churchill's 80th birthday, both Houses of Parliament presented Graham Sutherland's portrait to him in the Westminster Hall. Here he replies to the presentation address of Clement Attlee, leader of the Opposition.

After a dinner given for them by Queen Elizabeth in 1955, Sir Winston and the Commonwealth ministers pose for a formal photograph. From left, they are: Sir G. Huggins, Central African Federation; Mohammed Ali, Pakistan; R. Menzies, Australia; C. Swart, South African Minister of Justice; Sir Winston; S. Holland, New Zealand; L. St. Laurent, Canada; Pandit Nehru, India; Sir J. Kotelawala, Ceylon.

Churchill cited some of the "brutal facts" of that period and said, "Well may we humble ourselves and seek guidance and mercy."

He referred of course to nuclear weapons. Britain now possessed the secret of the hydrogen bomb and was prepared to build her own nuclear arsenal. Nobody at the time, including Churchill, could see precisely how the new weapons would affect military tactics and strategy, or whether in fact they might not have made war so terrible as to be unthinkable. Churchill expressed this thought in a speech in the House. "A curious paradox has emerged," he said. "After a certain point has been passed, it may be said that the worse things get, the better." On other occasions, he said, "We will have peace instead of roaming and peering around the edges of Hell." And, "We no longer live under the threat of war."

Rumors, possibly inspired, began to circulate that he would soon retire. He said they were "delusions." In the House, he sometimes dozed off to sleep. His memory appeared to be failing. With another General Election not far off, the Conservative leaders no doubt felt that a younger and more vigorous hand would be needed at the helm. Churchill, however, not only remained in office; he let it be known that he was busy on another broad canvas, *The History of the English Speaking Peoples*.

Like most men after having passed a certain point in life, Churchill did not like birthdays.

However, his eightieth, in 1954, was a great occasion and it deeply moved him. Both Houses of Parliament honored him in a special ceremony. Among their gifts was a portrait by Graham Sutherland, one of Britain's finest painters, which shows him in the House, hands clasping the arms of his chair, lower lip protruding, a thoughtful expression, in one of his most typical poses. Of the ceremonies in Parliament, Churchill said, "This is the most memorable public occasion of my life." He grew nostalgic and continued, "I have lived my life in the House of Commons, having served there for fifty-two out of the last fifty-four years of this tumultuous and convulsive century."

All day long, and from all parts of the world, messages and gifts poured in on him. One was from a man four years older than he, his friend, Bernard Baruch in New York. Baruch sent a telerecording, wishing him a happy birthday and noting that the Prime Minister had been a redoubtable success except in one long-term effort

—beating Baruch at gin rummy. Baruch said, however, "But you will win, Winston. You are younger than I and youth will prevail."

The photographer who took the eightieth-birthday portrait said, as he was packing his equipment, "Sir Winston, I expect to be here to take your picture on your one-hundredth birthday." Churchill eyed him for a long moment and replied, "I don't shee any reason why you shouldn't. You look perfectly hale and hearty."

Five months later, April 5, 1955, he resigned. The London newspapers were blacked out by a strike at the time but the word spread that he had had an audience with the Queen. Coupled with the speculation about his retirement, people suspected what had happened. Crowds gath-

The Queen and Duke of Edinburgh were guests at a dinner party given by Sir Winston and Lady Churchill at the Prime Minister's residence on April 4, 1955 at which Churchill's retirement was discussed. **Keystone Press**

On April 5, 1955 Churchill resigned. Anthony Eden, shown here with Sir Winston outside 10 Downing Street, became the new Conservative Prime Minister.

ered in front of Number 10 Downing Street and, calling for him, chanted "Good old Winnie." He threw back the window curtains and lifted his fingers in the V-sign. The demonstration continued for three hours. An intimate, not identified, said Churchill had decided several months earlier to resign because "he has a sort of dread at the idea of having to be carried out of 10 Downing Street."

That night, a great state dinner marked the end of his long tenure. Members of the Cabinet, Churchill's wartime associates in the Government, and the widow of Neville Chamberlain,

attended. So did the Queen and the Duke of Edinburgh, a rare event in British history.

Raising his glass to her, Churchill said, "I have the honor of proposing a toast which I used to enjoy drinking when I was a cavalry subaltern in the reign of Your Majesty's great-great grandmother, Queen Victoria."

Now indeed he had come to the end of his long journey, from the days of lance and sword to the hydrogen bomb, from the coach-and-four to jet airplanes. The great days were over and he had seen them bring the world to quieter waters.

SUNSET

CHURCHILL REMAINED IN THE House of Commons for nearly nine more years after he resigned as Prime Minister. A month after he left office, another General Election was called. Churchill was on a holiday in Sicily. He returned to campaign in his constituency, Woodford. At eighty-one, riding in a white automobile accompanied by "Clemmie," he took the stump with much if not all his old gusto. In the same year, he declined a Dukedom in order to retain his seat in the House. The proceedings there continued to be meat and drink to him. His volcanic life force began to ebb, in his mid-eighties but he occasionally raised his voice in the debates. He supported the action taken by his successor, Anthony Eden, in the Suez Crisis of 1956. And he drew on his vast experience to discuss the possibilities of a *detente* with the Soviet Union, and the meaning of the power shifts in the Kremlin in 1957. He said he detected "signs of decay" in Russian control over the Communist satellites several years before they came clearly into vision.

Meanwhile, at Chartwell, he wrote and painted. He finished his four-volume *History of the English Speaking Peoples* in 1958. His paintings, thirty-five in all, were exhibited in the United States, Canada, Australia and New Zealand. Some were hung in Britain's Royal Academy of Art, but they were not deemed worthy of exhibition in Chicago. In the same year, his horse, Welsh Abbott, won $8,400 in the Portland Handicap.

On his birthdays, the world honored him with mountains of messages and gifts. From early morning until past midnight, messengers would drive up to the gates of Chartwell. Sometimes, but not always, he went to the House of Commons and, as he entered, the Members on both sides rose and cheered. At home, there was always a cake, a big one, with a tribute in icing. On his eighty-third birthday, it said:

> We pass through Winter and hope for Spring
> And our ambitions are ever new;
> Of ambitious hopes we may yet sing
> While England has men like you.

After dinner and the dismantlement of the cake, there was brandy and the cigar. Churchill's

During a Conservative Club gathering in 1956, the former Prime Minister tried his hand at darts.

Sir Winston walks to the paddock to see his horse *Welsh Abbott* at Sandown Park in 1957.

Two "very old parties" (and old friends), Sir Winston and novelist W. Somerset Maugham, who were born a few months apart, relax outside Maugham's villa at Cap Ferrat, on the French Riviera in the Spring of 1959.

British Information Services

Churchill, accompanied by Field Marshal Montgomery of Alamein, walks past the new statue of himself then recently unveiled at Woodford, Essex. In bronze and standing nine feet high, the statue was the work of the young British sculptor David McFall and was erected in Sir Winston's honor by the constituents of Wanstead and Woodford which Churchill represented in Parliament for thirty-five years. More than £5,000 was raised for the statue by public subscription.

President Eisenhower holds on to the arm of Sir Winston as the elder British Statesman bids goodbye to the First Lady on the North Portico of the White House after spending several days as a guest at the executive mansion in 1959.

Wide World Photo

In his sunset years, Sir Winston often vacationed on the Mediterranean. He is shown with his friend Aristotle Onassis on a pause at Delphi during a cruise on Onassis' yacht, and in various moods.

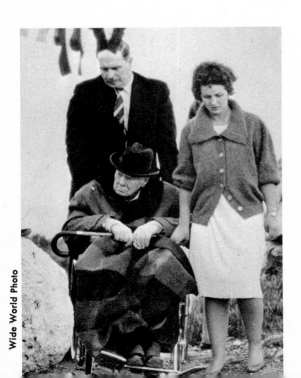

Randolph Churchill, on April 9, 1963, reads a message from his father at a White House ceremony in Washington. This followed President Kennedy's proclaiming Sir Winston an honorary citizen of the United States. Randolph's son Winston is at center, Mrs. Kennedy to his left.

On his 90th birthday, November 30, 1964, tributes poured in to Sir Winston from all over the world. Here crowds singing *For He's A Jolly Good Fellow,* gather outside his home at Hyde Park Gate. He greets them at the window.

strength was ebbing, but not his appetite for good things to eat and drink. "Winston's tastes are simple," said one of his friends, "he likes only the best."

In 1959, nearing eighty-five, he again campaigned in the General Election. He stayed up until after midnight to hear the returns and then went out and shook hands with his Laborite opponent, Arthur Latham. When Churchill returned to his seat after this election, he was named "Father of the House of Commons." He had then held a place there for thirty-five consecutive years.

Also in that year he came to the United States and was President Eisenhower's guest in the White House. Two years later he returned as a private guest.

But age was now rapidly overtaking him. He had attacks of bronchitis and pleurisy several times. He broke his hip while on a vacation in the Mediterranean. He had good days and bad. Sometimes, his friends said, his mind seemed to wander as though he had lost touch with reality.

He was not able to go to the House on his eighty-eighth birthday in 1962. But he appeared the next year, riding in his chromium-plated wheelchair. He also made a speech, urging the Government to keep its independent nuclear "deterrent."

His physical powers failed but his sense of humor endured. During the Bermuda Conference in 1953, he was asked why he had not attended church on a Sunday. He replied, "I will meet my Maker soon enough." Later, he embroidered the thought and said, "I am ready to meet my Maker but whether He is ready for the ordeal of meeting me is another matter."

In 1963, by Act of Congress, he became the first Honorary Citizen of the United States. Five years earlier, when the honor was offered, he had replied to President Eisenhower, "I feel that I would prefer to leave the matter thus rather than have an official seal put on the affection and high regard in which I hold your country." He did not come to Washington for the ceremony but he watched it on "live" television, bounced off the satellite, Telstar. Tears filled his eyes. He wrote President Kennedy:

"I have received many kindnesses from the United States of America, but the honour which you now accord me is without parallel. I accept it with deep gratitude and affection."

Finally, on May 2, 1963, the old warrior sheathed his sword forever.

He notified the Members of the House of Commons that he could not continue to serve with them. "I need not tell you with what sadness I feel constrained to take this step," he said. "I have now had the honour and privilege of sitting in the House of Commons for more than sixty years; for thirty-nine of these I have represented Epping and Woodford. Among the many aspects and chapters of my public life, it is my tenure as Member of Parliament that I value most highly."

One year and six months later, he celebrated his ninetieth birthday. The newspaper photographs clearly showed the ravages of age but his eyes looked bright and he could still manage a broad smile.

GOODNIGHT, THEN

Sᴜɴᴅᴀʏ, ᴊᴀɴᴜᴀʀʏ 24, ᴅᴀᴡɴᴇᴅ in London a gray and gloomy day. Wisps of mist shrouded the trees in Hyde Park, like white veils snagged in the branches. Raindrops trickled down the windows of the house at No. 28 Hyde Park Gate.

At 7:18, an automobile turned into the street bringing Lord Moran, the physician. He was fumbling with the door handle even before the car stopped at No. 28. He stepped quickly into the house. In a rear bedroom on the ground floor, wearing a green bed jacket, lay the man to whom he had ministered for many years, Sir Winston Churchill.

Soon after, the bell in St. Paul's Cathedral, known as "Great Tom," began tolling. Usually, it rings only to announce the death of royalty or the Lord Mayor of London. Then, over the radio, came a haunting echo of the Second World War, the opening notes of Beethoven's Fifth Symphony. Like three dots and a dash they would spell "V" in the Morse code. "V for Victory." The signal went out regularly from London to the countries occupied by the Germans during the war.

And so, even before Lord Moran's last bulletin was broadcast, people guessed that Churchill had gone. The bulletin, issued at 8:35, said, "Shortly after 8 ᴀ.ᴍ. this morning, Sunday, 24th January, Sir Winston Churchill died at his London home."

The death certificate, filed later with the Registrar in South Kensington, gave Churchill's occupation as "Statesman." It identified as the causes of death, "I A—cerebral thrombosis, B—cerebral arteriosclerosis; II—congestion of lungs."

January 24, 1965. Seventy years earlier, to the day, on January 24, 1895, Churchill's father, Lord Randolph, had died.

The end came on the tenth day after Churchill was stricken with his final illness. On Friday, January 15, Lord Moran and Lord Brain, a neurologist, had been summoned. They issued a terse bulletin which merely said Churchill was "unwell." Three hours later, they announced he had suffered a cerebral thrombosis—a stroke. As the days passed, succeeding bulletins contained the words "deteriorated" or "weakened." One said he had passed into a deep sleep "and feels no pain or discomfort whatever."

He slipped away gradually and gently. And so the millions who cherished him were prepared for this. There was no occasion for shock or surprise. He was past ninety and the world could offer nothing more for him. Churchill might have been speaking of his own passing when he said, at the funeral of King George VI, "He fell asleep as every man or woman who strives to fear God and nothing else in the world may hope to do."

His "darling Clementine," their son, Randolph, and daughters, Mary and Sarah, were beside him when he breathed his last.

Crowds began gathering in Trafalgar Square, the great open expanse in the heart of London. Clergymen intoned prayers over a microphone placed at the base of the tall column erected in honor of Lord Nelson. Soon the number became so great that there was no more room in the Square and the steps of the National Gallery, some distance from the column, filled with people come to pay their respects in this way.

Meanwhile, the news having flashed around the world, messages were pouring in on London from the heads of state in many nations.

At the news of Sir Winston's grave illness, on January 15, 1965, somber throngs gather outside his home at 28 Hyde Park Gate, London, awaiting news of the old warrior's condition.

Newsmen and Londoners continue the ten-day-long vigil outside Churchill's home. His daughters Mary and Sarah, his son Randolph and grandson Winston made frequent visits to his bedside. The Archbishop of Canterbury called upon his countrymen to offer their prayers for Sir Winston, "whose work is done and the end of whose life is near."

Lord Moran, personal physician to Sir Winston for many years, read frequent medical bulletins to members of the press crowded outside 28 Hyde Park Gate. Years earlier Lord Moran had said of his old friend: "More than once I have been with him when news of reverses was brought to him, and in my heart I have come to think of him as invincible."

After the announcement of Sir Winston's death on January 24, crowds continued to mill about near Churchill's residence. Tributes to the former Prime Minister, which poured in from all over the world, included this from W. Somerset Maugham, himself almost 91: "We have lost the greatest man of our time and personally I have lost an old friend—and I'm extremely unhappy."

Women stood weeping outside the Churchill home after news of the statesman's passing. Editorially, *The New York Times* said: "The power and the glory are gone, the soaring oratory, the eloquent pen, the cherubic face, the impish twinkle in the eyes, the jaunty cigar, the vitality that sparked a world."

Boys of Harrow School at Harrow-on-the-Hill, Middlesex, remove their straw hats as a mark of respect as they view the school flag flying at half staff after the death of Sir Winston, the school's most famous "old boy."

For three days Sir Winston's body lay in state in Westminster Hall, London. Members of the public file slowly past his flag-draped coffin. Mounting watch around the bier are Royal Horse and Life Guards (left). The line of mourners stretched for two miles.

Lyndon Baines Johnson, hospitalized with a heavy cold, cabled from Washington, "The people of the United States—his cousins and fellow citizens—will pray with his British countrymen for God's eternal blessing on this man, and for comfort to his family. He is history's child, and what he said and what he did will never die." Johnson said he hoped to be able to attend Churchill's funeral, but in the end, on the advice of his doctors, he did not go to London.

President Charles De Gaulle said in a message to Queen Elizabeth, "For all in my country and for myself, Sir Winston is, and will forever remain, the one who in directing to final victory the admirable effort of Great Britain contributed powerfully to the salvation of the French people and to the liberty of the world."

Frenchmen recalled a radio broadcast directed to them by Churchill in 1940 after they had been defeated by the Germans. Speaking in French, with the accent he himself would joke about, he said:

"Good night, then; sleep to gather strength for the morning, for the morning will come.

Brightly will it shine on the brave and true, the kindly, on all who suffer for the cause, and gloriously upon the tombs of heroes. Thus will shine the dawn."

Pope Paul VI addressed his message to Lady Churchill, "We offer our profound sympathy on the passing of your beloved husband, Sir Winston Churchill, great statesman, and indefatigable champion of freedom, independence and peace."

Hour after hour, from all corners of the globe, such tributes poured in, to the Queen, to Lady Churchill, to Prime Minister Harold Wilson. There was little anyone could say about Churchill that had not been said while he lived. Yet, his death was the occasion for restating the most important fact of his life: That he had led the fight against the twin tyrannies of Nazism and Communism, and that to him, more than to any other individual, the Free nations owed their freedom.

Even his enemies, the Germans, Russians, Japanese and Irish, added their voices to the swelling chorus.

From Moscow, Premier Aleksei N. Kosygin

The coffin passes the Houses of Parliament and Big Ben en route from Westminster Hall to St. Paul's Cathedral for funeral services, January 30.

Londoners measured Sir Winston's greatness in their hundreds of thousands as the funeral procession made its way to St. Paul's.

telegraphed, "The tireless efforts of Sir Winston during the war against Hitlerite Germany are remembered in the Soviet Union, and the grief of the British people in this bereavement is shared here."

Churchill, who constantly urged magnanimity in victory, would have approved the statement issued by Karl Gunther von Hase, chief spokesman for the West German Government. Von Hase said Churchill "was an implacable enemy of Germany during the war but he remained true to his principles by becoming the first of the victorious leaders to stretch out the hand of peace and turn to the task of unifying Europe."

The Japanese Premier, Eisaku Sato, called Churchill "the most outstanding and famous personality of the present century." He immediately began selecting a delegation to represent Japan at the funeral.

In Ireland, with its ancient hostility toward the English, the *Irish Press* said, "He was not our friend, but the bitterness of battle is now dissolved in the universal solvent of humanity . . . We join in the universal tribute to his memory."

In Lagos, the Nigerian Radio broadcast a half hour of funeral music and then recapitulated the principal events in Churchill's life in a program called *The End of a Legend.* Argentina declared a day of mourning. In New York, he United Nations flag was lowered to half-staff. The New York Philharmonic played a selection in his memory, a long, slow passage from Sir Edward Elgar's *Enigma,* and the audience stood.

Across the United States, as millions of Americans assembled in their churches that Sunday morning, Protestant, Catholic and Jewish clergymen reverently spoke of Churchill. Television networks devoted long programs to the great moments of his life. And in thousands of newspaper offices, editors began putting into type the stirring passages from his speeches. A whole generation of Americans had grown to maturity in the twenty-five years since the Second World War, and to most of them, Churchill was only a name, an indistinct figure. Now, in death, he became vividly alive for them.

On Monday, January 25, the massive outpouring of feeling became even more impressive. Queen Elizabeth sent a message to the House

Watched by family mourners at left, the bearer party Grenadier Guards carry the coffin up the steps of St. Pau for funeral services. Heading the mourners are La Clementine Churchill and her son Randolph. Seen behi them are daughters Sarah, Lady Audley (left, partly hidde and Mrs. Mary Soames, standing in front of her husban Christopher Soames.

More than 100 sailors of the Royal Navy—Sir Winston's favorite service—draw the gun carriage and its burden at a measured 65 paces to the minute through Trafalgar Square on the way to St. Paul's.

The funeral procession files down the center aisle of St. Paul's in a view taken from the Whispering Gallery.

The coffin rests on the catafalque during the State Funeral of Sir Winston. At the close of the service, a Royal Horse Guards trumpeter sounded the *Last Post* from the Whispering Gallery, and in answer from across the cathedral came the bugle call of *Reveille* played by a Royal Irish Hussar.

of Commons advising the Members that she had ordered a State funeral for Churchill. In it, she said:

"Confident that I can rely upon the support of my faithful Commons and upon their liberality in making suitable provision for the proper discharge of our debt of gratitude and tribute of national sorrow, I have directed that Sir Winston's body shall lie in State in Westminster Hall and that thereafter the funeral shall be held in the Cathedral Church of St. Paul's."

In this, the procedure was reversed from the last time a commoner was granted a State funeral. William Ewart Gladstone, four times Prime Minister, died in 1898 and on that occasion it was the House of Commons that petitioned Queen Victoria to grant him the honor. Gladstone, for all his political stature, had never charmed the Queen.

Having read Elizabeth's message, Prime Minister Wilson then proceeded with his Eulogy of Churchill.

The House was packed. There was one empty place, the green leather seat on the front bench just below the gangway. This had been Churchill's. In a moving passage, Wilson pictured Churchill on this scene—

> As Parliament succeeded Parliament, he stood at this box, at one time or another, holding almost every one of the great offices of State. He stood at the box opposite, thundering his denunciations of Government after Government. He sat on the bench opposite, below the gangway, disregarded, seemingly impotent, finished.
>
> Each one of us recalls some little incident—many of us, as in my own case, a kind of action graced with the courtesy of a past generation and going far beyond the calls of Parliamentary comradeship.

Wilson closed by saying that Churchill would have chosen as his epitaph, "He was a good House of Commons man."

A low, rumbling sound, "Hear, hear," sounded from both sides of the House.

On the same day, newspapers published the poem in honor of Churchill written by John Masefield, the Poet Laureate. The last stanza said:

Or, speaking, uttered like the very breed
Of Francis Drake, disaster being near,
One solemn watchword, to have done with fear.
Thence, without other drumbeat, all took cheer,
Content with such a Captain, such a creed.

The front page of the London *Times* normally carries only classified advertisments. On that Monday, the editors gave over Page One to Churchill, with the caption, "The Greatest Englishman of His Time." *The New York Herald Tribune* also devoted the whole of its front page to Churchill and called that day's newspaper "Churchill Memorial Edition." *The New York Times* published an eight-page supplement tracing his life and works.

The United Nations General Assembly, representatives of 115 countries, stood in a moment of silence. At 11 A.M., the customary clamor and bustle of the two Stock Exchanges in New York suddenly ceased. For two minutes, trading was interrupted and utter silence filled the great chambers.

Other Americans took the trouble to go to the British Consulate-General, on the eleventh floor of a building in New York, to pay their respects to Churchill. On a table covered with black velvet, beside a framed picture of the old statesman, a Book of Condolence lay open. A queue soon formed. By Tuesday, more than 3,000 signatures had gone into the book and the time was extended for another day. One of the first to inscribe his name was a street cleaner.

Meanwhile, in London, everything was ready for the great State funeral. The Duke of Norfolk, who had arranged the complicated details for the Coronation of Elizabeth II, said preparations for Churchill's funeral were complete "because of information I received some time ago." He did not elaborate.

However, it was reported that Churchill himself had planned the details of his funeral. One commentator said (as related in Air Vice Marshal Kelly's diary) that he did this in North Africa during the war while he was convalescing from the bout with pneumonia.

At 9:15, on the night of January 26, a hearse bore Churchill's body from Hyde Park Gate to Westminster Hall. The Lord Chamberlain, Lord Cobbold, Master of the Queen's House, escorted

Sir Winston's coffin begins its procession down the aisle as the great bells of St. Paul's peal out.

Lady Churchill takes the arm of her son Randolph, at the head of the family mourners, as they follow the coffin out of the cathedral. The vast congregation of 3,000 was headed by Queen Elizabeth II and included the representatives of 110 countries. Seen behind Lady Churchill are her daughters, Sarah—left—and Mary (Mrs. Christopher Soames), Randolph Churchill's son Winston, his wife Minnie, and at extreme right, Christopher Soames.

it. Lady Churchill, heavily veiled, and accompanied by her children and grandchildren, followed in limousines. At the Hall, eight Grenadier Guardsmen carried the coffin to a catafalque. Here, for the next three days, the body lay in state.

No building in England evokes the majestic sweep of British history more powerfully than Westminster Hall. It was built in 1099 by King William Rufus, who held his first court there. The hammer-beamed Gothic roof, spanning more than sixty-seven feet without supports, has been called "a miracle."

The Hall breathes of tragedy and drama. Having been the seat of the chief law court of England for a long period, it was the scene of the trials of Richard II, Charles I, Queen Caroline, Sir Thomas More, Warren Hasting of India, and Titus Oates, accused of conspiracy. Oliver Cromwell took the Oath here. Wellington's funeral recalled the Napoleonic Era. And in the Age of Churchill, German bombs damaged the ancient structure. Churchill personified John Bull in his day, and Westminster Hall, for nearly nine centuries has personified Great Britain.

At nine o'clock, on the morning of Wednesday, January 27, Big Ben's deep voice boomed across London. The huge clock is in the Palace of Westminster, adjacent to Westminster Hall.

The huge oaken doors opened. Prime Minister Wilson entered. Thousands already were queued up, waiting in the bitter cold to enter the Hall.

Towering over the closed coffin was a golden cross, sparkling in the light of six candles ensconced in giant candlesticks, at each corner of the bier and at the head and foot. A Union Jack covered the coffin. Churchill's insignia as a Knight of the Garter was placed on a black cushion on top of the cushion.

The Prime Minister and his wife stopped beside the catafalque, bowed toward it, and walked outside. Herbert Bowden, Leader of the House of Commons, followed. Then came the Peers and Members of the House of Commons. In the first group to appear was Field Marshal Lord Alexander of Tunis, one of Churchill's greatest military leaders during the Second World War.

It was a gray, cold morning. A northeast wind, threatening snow, whipped in from the North Sea.

Nevertheless, thousands of people already were lined up in the streets, waiting to enter. One young man, Nicholas Hutchins, said he had been waiting throughout the night. "I think Sir Winston was the greatest man the world has ever known," he said. "I thought the least I could do was to wait, before going through, as a mark of respect." An eighty-one-year-old woman, Mrs. Ellen Lewin, said she had walked from her home in Notting Hill. It is about three miles from the Hall. "That was nothing," she said. "But this is something—I'm proud to have been born in the Churchill Era."

Outside, the line was growing longer. At times it stretched away from the Hall for nearly two miles.

During the three days of lying-in-state, it was estimated that more than 300,000 people filed past the catafalque. The costumes of Asia and Africa were seen in the lines. Invalids in wheel chairs were brought to the scene, and even the blind came.

Queen Elizabeth entered the Hall Thursday night, setting a precedent. It was the first of several in these last rites. With the Queen were the Duke of Edinburgh, her husband, and Princess Margaret and her husband, the Earl of Snowdon.

Queen Victoria did not attend on the last two occasions when the bodies of commoners lay-in-state in the Hall, the funerals of the Duke of Wellington in 1852 and Gladstone in 1898.

Lady Churchill and her daughters came several times to the catafalque. Once they stayed twenty minutes, watching the changing of the guards.

Meanwhile, in Berlin and Washington, special services were being held in Churchill's memory. Heinrich Lubke, President of West Germany, led the services in Berlin, which were attended by 2,000 German and Allied officials. Thus, his former enemies repaid him for "magnanimity in victory."

In the huge Washington Cathedral, Adlai Stevenson delivered the American eulogy of Churchill. Vice-President Humphrey and his wife, and President Johnson's elder daughter, Lynda, were among the 3,000 who attended. 115

Harold Wilson, the Prime Minister, and Mrs. Wilson are shown in the procession of distinguished mourners filing out of the cathedral at the conclusion of services.

Members of the British Royal Family pause on the steps of St. Paul's after the funeral service. From left to right and front to rear, are: Queen Elizabeth II and Prince Philip; Queen Mother Elizabeth and Prince Charles, Prince of Wales; Princess Margaret and her husband Lord Snowdon; the Duchess and Duke of Gloucester and the Princess Royal; the sons of the Duke and Duchess of Gloucester, Prince William and Prince Richard, and the Duchess of Kent.

The President was still confined to the White House with a cold. Stevenson said:

> In the last analysis, all the zest and life and confidence of this incomparable man sprang, I believe, not only from the rich endowment of his nature but also from a profound and simple faith in God. In the prime of his powers, confronted with the apocalyptic risks of annihilation, he said serenely, 'I do not believe that God has despaired of his people.'
>
> We shall hear no longer the remembered eloquence and wit, the old courage and defiance, the robust serenity of indomitable faith. Our world is thus poorer, our political dialogue is diminished and the sources of public inspiration run more thinly for all of us.
>
> There is a lonesome place against the sky.

Stevenson's voice faltered several times as he spoke.

All the many evidences of American affection and respect for Churchill's memory—the unparalleled newspaper space and television time devoted to the last rites, the many eulogies and special services in American churches—would have cheered him mightily. One of the cardinal principles of his political philosophy was a close relationship between Britain and the United States. He strove mightily toward this goal. What he accomplished in life now seemed fully reflected in the great expression of American feeling at his death.

Dwight D. Eisenhower touched on this note in a broadcast in London on the day of Churchill's funeral. In his tribute, he recalled his wartime association with Churchill, and then he said:

> The war ended, our friendship flowered in the later and more subtle tests imposed by international politics. Then, each of us, holding high official post in his own nation, strove together so to concert the strength of our two peoples that liberty might be preserved among men and the security of the Free World wholly sustained.

In Paris, there were more special ceremonies in honor of Churchill, and these were tinged with a bitterness he would not have shared. They were conducted in the Church of St. Louis, part of the Invalides, the military shrine, site of Napoleon's Tomb.

General Maxime Weygand, Army commander when France capitulated in 1940, had died. The Government refused permission for his funeral to be held in the Church of St. Louis.

Churchill wrote of the events of 1940, "Weygand had convinced [Marshal Henri] Petain without much difficulty that England was lost. High French military authorities—perhaps Weygand himself—had advised: 'In three weeks, England will have her neck wrung like a chicken.' " Churchill liked to recall these words. In a speech in the Canadian Parliament, he said, after a pause and a sly wink, "Some chicken. Some neck." He wept openly when the French decided to ask for an armistice. But he held no bitterness. He quarrelled often in London with General Charles DeGaulle, leader of the Free French, whose insignia was the Cross of Lorraine. "Every man has his cross to bear," Churchill said. "Mine is the Cross of Lorraine." Yet he was one of the first to ride down the Champs Elysées in Paris with DeGaulle when victory came in 1945.

Saturday, January 30, 1965, the day of the memorable funeral . . .

By a strange coincidence, history already marks this date, through the lives of three men with whom Churchill's life was entwined. On January 30, 1882, Franklin D. Roosevelt was born. On this date in 1933, Adolf Hitler became Chancellor of the German Reich. On January 30, 1948, Mohandas K. Gandhi was assassinated in New Delhi.

It was a cold day in London, overcast, with a threat of snow. People lining the processional route wrapped newspapers under their coats.

At 9:45, Big Ben chimed, signalling the start of the great funeral procession. The bell remained silent through the rest of the day.

On the minute, the gun carriage bearing the coffin moved out, drawn by 142 men of the Royal Navy. The gun carriage, before this, had never transported the body of a commoner. As for the tradition of sailors drawing it, the story is that, during Queen Victoria's funeral, the horses grew skittish, interrupting the procession. It is said that William I, Emperor of Germany, suggested unhitching the horses and having the detachment of sailors escorting the carriage draw it.

Wide World Photos

President Charles DeGaulle of France, in the uniform of a Brigadier General, stands with the other mourners on the steps of St. Paul's. In front of him are Princess Marina and her sons, Prince Michael (left), and the Duke of Kent. Behind the Duke, Queen Juliana of the Netherlands speaks to her husband, Prince Bernhard.

Two former British Prime Ministers, Harold Macmillan (left center) and Lord Avon (formerly Sir Anthony Eden, right center), gather outside St. Paul's after the funeral. Immediately behind Lord Avon is David Ben-Gurion, former Israeli Premier. In front of Lord Avon is Lord Bridges. Just to the right of him is former British Prime Minister Lord Attlee.

Wide World Photos

The procession stretched across more than a mile.

But it stretched much farther in time. The heralds clad in gold, red and blue with black sashes, the regiments with famous names and the naval units from renowned ships, the skirling bagpipes and trumpeters, the flags and pennons—here were many centuries of Britain's glorious history.

The line of march went from the Hall of Kings in Westminster, up Whitehall, through Trafalgar Square, along the Strand into Fleet Street, and down Ludgate Hill to St. Paul's Cathedral where the last rites were held. This route took Churchill's body past buildings where he lived some of his greatest hours, the Houses of Parliament and the Government offices in Whitehall. In Fleet Street, a number of London's leading newspapers have their offices and it was in the newspapers, in effect, where he made his start.

The gun carriage came toward the rear of the procession.

Ahead of it marched the heralds—Windsor bearing a sword, Somerset a shield showing the family coat-of-arms, York the herald spurs, symbol of knighthood, and Lancaster, a figure of a lion, the crest from Churchill's stall in the Chapel of the Garter at Windsor Castle.

The Earl Marshal, Duke of Norfolk, preceded the family. The white feathers of his cocked hat rippled in the wind. Randolph Churchill, his son, and the other male members of the family came next on foot. Lady Churchill and her daughters, Sarah (Lady Audley) and Mrs. Mary Soames, rode in the Queen's carriages. They sat very straight, a picture of courage in an hour of ordeal.

At least a million people watched them pass. The vast throng was quiet. All London was quiet.

At one-minute intervals, ninety guns were fired, one for each year of Churchill's life. Twelve bands played funeral music, setting the slow cadence for the marchers. Drums were muffled. The officers and troops marched with swords and rifles reversed.

On the steps of St. Paul's, as the cortege came up, stood Queen Elizabeth. This, too, was a precedent.

From St. Paul's Cathedral the coffin was borne away on the shoulders of Guards officers to the gun carriage (out of picture at right) to Tower Pier for the river journey to Waterloo Railway Station. Leaving down the center steps are relatives of Sir Winston.

The twelve pallbearers fell in behind the tall Cross of Canterbury. Three had been Prime Minister, Earl Attlee, Harold MacMillan, and Lord Avon (Anthony Eden.)

Inside the Cathedral, 3,000 mourners from 110 nations waited. Among them were King Frederik IX of Denmark, King Olav V of Norway, King Baudoin of Belgium, Queen Juliana of the Netherlands, King Constantine of Greece, and Grand Duke Jean of Luxembourg.

DeGaulle and Eisenhower sat near one another in the Cathedral. The French President wore the uniform of a brigadier-general, with one star, his rank at the beginning of World War II. Seventeen other nations were represented by Presidents, Premiers, Chancellors and Prime Ministers, a number of them accompanied by their Foreign Ministers. Nobosuke Kishi, former Premier of Japan, represented his country and the Soviet Union sent Marshal Ivan S. Konev, a World War II commander, and Deputy Premier Konstantin N. Rudnev.

The Archbishop of Canterbury, Dr. Michael Ramsey, walked down an aisle in the Cathedral promptly at 10 A.M. Dignitaries then entered bringing the golden maces of the House of Commons and House of Lords. Most of the other mourners already were in their places by that time.

Eight Grenadier Guards, having removed their tall bearskin shakos, lifted the coffin from the gun carriage and brought it slowly down the main aisle. Lady Churchill and her children followed.

The first hymn began with the words:

"Who would true valor see, let him come hither."

Other hymns followed. Then the Dean of St. Paul's, Dr. N. R. Matthews, entered the pulpit and prayed for Churchill:

"We shall think of him with thanksgiving that he was raised up in our days of desperate need to be a leader and inspirer of the nation, for his dauntless resolution and untiring vigilance and for his example of courage and endurance."

The Archbishop of Canterbury, robed in red emblazoned with the Queen's seal, asked the Lord's Blessing for Churchill. A low "Amen" rumbled through the high-domed Cathedral from the mourners, kneeling.

The coffin is carried aboard the Port of London Launch *Havengore* to the piping of a bo'sun's whistle.   Wide World Photos

Then came a uniquely American note in this British State funeral. The organ burst into the stirring strains of "The Battle Hymn of the Republic," which Churchill himself had requested for his funeral. It had been sung at the funeral of Abraham Lincoln.

After the singing of "God Save the Queen," silence filled the Cathedral. Then, from a gallery high under the dome, came the plangent notes of a trumpet, sounding "The Last Post." The trumpeter's costume was medieval. A pennon hung from the trumpet. Another trumpet answered, playing "Reveille." The trumpeter was of the Royal Hussars.

So the service ended.

The Grenadiers lifted the coffin and bore it again to the gun carriage in the streets. The Queen, Prince Philip, Kings, Presidents and Prime Ministers assembled. As the gun carriage moved away, going to a pier near the Tower of London in the Thames, the male mourners saluted.

Churchill's body then was placed on an eighty-five-foot launch, *Havengore,* for transport down the Thames to another pier, and then to Waterloo Station. A battery of old guns along the river, nineteen in all, gave him another last salute. Commoners normally receive a seventeen-gun salute on these occasions. The coffin was piped aboard the launch, also a precedent for a civilian. As it moved away from the pier, a band of the 41st Royal Marines broke into "Rule Britannia."

Now the sad drama was moving into its last act.

Churchill's body was taken by train from London to the village of Bladon. He could have had his remains interred in Westminster Abbey. However, he chose the little village graveyard of St. Martin's Church where his parents are buried. The church is within sight of Blenheim Palace, his birthplace.

At the entrance to the churchyard a small wooden bower bears the inscription, "I am the resurrection and the life." A simple stone cross stands at the head of Lord Randolph's grave. It bears the inscription, "Thy will be done." Churchill's brother, Jack, is buried here and so is the mother of the present Duke of Marlborough, the former Consuelo Vanderbilt who, like Churchill's mother, was an American. Blenheim's towers and turrets look down on the small church and cemetery from a distance.

The services here were private. They lasted only a few minutes. After the Reverend John James, Rector of St. Martin's, spoke the final funerary words, "Ashes to ashes . . . ," Lady Churchill sprinkled earth on the grave.

The long day of pomp and pageantry, the muffled drums and funeral music, the glittering helmets, breastplates, uniforms and decorations, the booming guns and the reverent silence of the crowds, the prayers and eulogies—the last rites for Winston Leonard Spencer Churchill, rites worthy of a King, were ended.

After the family left and the gates of the churchyard were opened, visitors found at the head of the new grave a wreath of red roses, tulips and carnations.

The ribbon on it said, "To my darling Winston. Clemmie."

A classic Greek precept holds that happiness is derived from the full exercise of a man's powers and capabilities "in a life affording them scope."

By that definition, Winston Churchill died a happy and fulfilled man.

He was a writer and his writings won wide acclaim. He was an orator and he saw how his mighty words steeled and inspired his people in the hour of peril. He was a politician and he twice fought his way to Britain's highest office. He was a statesman and he saw two great objectives come closer to being achieved, closer relations with the United States and the beginnings of unity in Europe. Above all, he was an Englishman and he went to his grave knowing that he had served England well.

He did not prevent "the liquidation of the British Empire." No man could have stood against the powerful tides of nationalism in the world after World War II.

Nor did he win "the last great prize," the end of the ideological war between East and West. Yet, in Moscow, the Deputy Foreign Minister, Valerian A. Zorin, and a group of Russian officials attended memorial services in his honor. And in Poland, all eight national television stations brought direct transmission of the scenes

"The last great Englishman is low." Crowds queue up outside St. Martin's Churchyard in Bladon to file past the grave of Sir Winston, who was buried close by his birthplace at Blenheim.

"Such was he: his work is done. . . . Eternal honour to his name."

of his funeral to their audiences. So perhaps in this field of relations with the Communists, he made a contribution the fruits of which may be apparent later.

Shakespeare had Hamlet say of his father as we may say of Winston Churchill—

"He was a man, take him for all in all. I shall not look upon his like again."

CHRONOLOGY

1874—Born at Blenheim Palace, November 30.

1887–94—Educated at Harrow and Royal Military Academy, Sandhurst

1895—Lieutenant in the Queen's Fourth Hussars; in action in India and on the Nile.

1899—Defeated in first try for the House of Commons; captured in Boer War, escapes.

1900—Elected to Parliament as a Conservative.

1904—Bolts the Conservatives and joins the Liberals.

1906—Named Under-Secretary of State for Colonies.

1908—Named President of the Board of Trade; married, Sept. 12, to Clementine Ogilvy Hozier, daughter of Sir Henry Montague Hozier and Lady Henrietta Blanche, daughter of the seventh Earl of Airlie.

1909—Birth of Diana Churchill, July 11.

1910—Appointed Home Secretary.

1911—Appointed First Lord of the Admiralty; birth of Randolph Frederick Edward Churchill, May 28.

1914—Orders mobilization of the Fleet; World War I begins; birth of Sarah Millicent Hermione Churchill, October 7.

1915—Leaves the Admiralty after failure of the Dardanelles offensive.

1916—Commanding Sixth Royal Scots Fusiliers in France.

1917—Minister of Munitions.

1918—Secretary of State for War and for Air; birth of Marigold Frances Churchill, November 15, died August 23, 1921.

1919—Organizes British Expedition against Bolsheviks in Russia.

1921—Secretary for the Colonies.

1922—Leaves Liberal Party, defeated as an Independent in Parliamentary Elections; birth of Mary Churchill, September 15.

1923—Begins writing *The World Crisis,* history of World War I.

1924—Reelected to Parliament; Chancellor of the Exchequer to 1929.

1925—Rejoins Conservatives.

1929–39—Out of office.

1933—First warnings about German resurgence.

1936—Defends King Edward VIII in Parliamentary crisis over Mrs. Simpson.

1939—Returns as First Lord of the Admiralty.

1940—Prime Minister and Minister of Defense.

1941—Meets President Roosevelt; the Atlantic Charter; addresses U.S. Congress.

1941–45—Atends conferences in Washington, Moscow, Quebec, Cairo, Casablanca, Athens, Malta, Yalta, Teheran and Potsdam.

1945—Surrender of Germany; Churchill's Government falls in General Election.

1945–51—Leader of His Majesty's Loyal Opposition in Parliament.

1946—Delivers the "Iron Curtain" Speech in Fulton, Missouri; begins six-volume history of World War II.

1951—Begins second term as Prime Minister, October 26.

1953—Semi-paralyzed and rendered speechless by a stroke; awarded Nobel Prize for Literature; made Knight of the Garter by Queen Elizabeth II.

1954—Begins *History of the English Speaking Peoples.*

1955—Resigns as Prime Minister, April 5.

1959—Named "Father of the House of Commons."

1963—By Act of Congress, becomes the first Honorary Citizen of the United States; nearing ninety, he resigns from the House of Commons.

1964—Celebrates his ninetieth birthday.

1965—Dies in London, January 24, 1965. State Funeral, St. Paul's Cathedral, January 30.